Is it possible to say anything fresh or ⟨…⟩ and Christian complementarianism ⟨…⟩ thrashed out in countless essays ar⟨…⟩ painfully predictable, but each 'side' is convinced it has 'won'. Into this maelstrom of publications, Claire Smith's little book comes with a refreshing sanity, a happy eagerness to let Scripture speak, and a simple style that will frustrate the pundits and make many ordinary Christian readers rejoice over this breath of fresh air, this godly and biblically faithful call to rejoice in *God's Good Design*.

DA Carson
Research Professor of New Testament, Trinity Evangelical Divinity School, Deerfield

God's Good Design is a 'must buy, must read'!

It is a *must* for instinctive 'complementarians' who sometimes fumble over crucial texts. Claire Smith's unpacking of 1 Timothy 2 and 1 Corinthians 11 and 14 is faithful, lucid and compelling.

It is a *must* for 'egalitarians' to challenge them to front up to these texts. Their frequent objections are faced and answered.

It is a *must* for any church and denomination. There is a strong correlation between a healthy, growing church and the recognition of distinctive ministries for men and women. Where women usurp men's proper ministry and are not themselves given their own unique and vital ministry, churches frequently decline.

It is a *must* for our society. One of the greatest threats facing us today is the breakdown of marriage and family life. The exposition of Ephesians 5 and, wonderfully, of Proverbs 31 sets us on the road to recovery.

It is a must!

Jonathan Fletcher
Vicar of Emmanuel Church, Wimbledon

Claire Smith's fine scholarship makes her an excellent guide to the teaching of Scripture on the subject of men and women. She has a desire to be true to God's word and to show how God's word enhances human life. This is no abstract discussion—Claire has a rich and thoughtful experience of what she writes about. This is a book worth reading!

Peter Jensen
Anglican Archbishop of Sydney

Claire Smith tackles passages that some have claimed are 'too hard', and she does this with the clear conviction that this is God's good word to us. This is a helpful resource for the church because it works through the Bible passages verse by verse, letting them set the agenda for the ministry of men and women, rather than simply making assertions from elsewhere. It is evident throughout the book that Claire has been working on these texts for many years. She writes so plainly and clearly, and she addresses common objections and pastoral issues. This clarity makes the book widely accessible.

Jane M Tooher
Director of The Priscilla and Aquila Centre, Moore College, Sydney

Gallons of ink have been spilt over issues of male and female roles in church leadership and the home. Few authors have provided such a careful, accurate and convincing treatment of the biblical texts involved. This outstanding book is comprehensive, thoroughly readable, full of useful application and apologetic, and will provide us with a magnificent resource for our churches for many years to come. I could not commend it more highly!

William Taylor
Rector of St Helen's Bishopsgate, London

This book is a welcome addition to the 'gender' landscape. Claire Smith's careful and meticulous attention to the biblical text is of immense service to those who are not afraid to dig deep below the surface in order to fathom truth. This book is thorough, comprehensive and scholarly. I wholeheartedly recommend it to men and women who yearn to live within God's good design for relationships in church and family.

Lesley C Ramsay
Evangelist and Bible teacher, Sydney

This is a most loving contribution to the gender discussions of today. And we who follow Christ cannot afford to pretend the Bible is too difficult or debatable on these matters without losing traction on many others.

Claire Smith walks us through the biblical texts so intelligibly, winsomely, pertinently and persuasively that we have fresh cause to thank God and put his wise ways into practice.

Simon Manchester
Rector of St Thomas', North Sydney

Claire Smith's thoughtful, careful work deserves a full read from beginning to end. She aims not to advance an argument but to listen well to God's word about men and women and their relationships with each other. This book models some of the most important exegetical principles: close attention to the Bible's words; study of texts in their immediate and full contexts; consistent effort to say no more or less than the Bible says; and personal humility and joy in receiving God's word. I commend this book not as a checklist for a view but as a worthy guide along the path of listening well to God's voice in Scripture.

Kathleen B Nielson
Author and conference speaker, Georgia

God's Good Design stands alone as a succinct yet comprehensive exploration of the Bible's teaching on men and women. Claire Smith's attention to detail and ability to apply God's word to our lives means this book will sharpen our thinking and enrich the lives of men and women regardless of age, stage in life or cultural background. Without hesitation, I recommend *God's Good Design* as a 'must read' for every Christian.

Carmelina Read
Chair of EQUIP ministry women conference, Sydney

This is a great book that systematically lays out all God says on this important issue. It is thorough, comprehensive, accessible and compelling. It avoids the trap of saying more than God has said, but carefully says no less. It therefore confronts men as well as women and calls us back to God's good design.

And it's helpful to have an author who can so sensitively engage with such depth on so profound a topic in the context of truly knowing the pain and gain of wrestling with these things! Read the last chapter first. It helps to keep in mind who it is that writes.

I'll be one of the first to stock this important, relevant and careful book in our church bookshop.

Andrew Heard
Lead Pastor, EV Church, Erina

GOD'S GOOD DESIGN

WHAT THE BIBLE REALLY SAYS
ABOUT MEN AND WOMEN

GOD'S GOOD DESIGN

WHAT THE BIBLE REALLY SAYS ABOUT MEN AND WOMEN

CLAIRE SMITH

God's Good Design
© Matthias Media 2012

Matthias Media
(St Matthias Press Ltd ACN 067 558 365)
PO Box 225
Kingsford NSW 2032
Australia
Telephone: (02) 9233 4627; international: +61 2 9233 4627
Email: info@matthiasmedia.com.au
Internet: www.matthiasmedia.com.au

Matthias Media (USA)
Telephone: 330 953 1702; international: +1 330 953 1702
Email: sales@matthiasmedia.com
Internet: www.matthiasmedia.com

ISBN 978 1 921441 39 2

Cover design and typesetting by Lankshear Design.

CONTENTS

To my dear husband, Rob

PREFACE

ANYONE VAGUELY FAMILIAR with the question of the roles and relationships of men and women in the church and in marriage will know there is already no shortage of books on the subject. So why the need for another?

The answer is that this book is not focused on arguing one side or the other of an *issue*—like women's ordination or women's ministry or the best model for modern marriages. I will address these matters, of course, but they are not the main focus.

The main focus is the *Bible passages* that should determine these issues. This book is a text-by-text, verse-by-verse, and sometimes word-by-word look at passages that many of us have put in the 'too hard basket' or made up our minds about years ago and not revisited since. It is the sort of close Bible study we must do if we are to know and love the wisdom of God's purposes for men and women.

For the most part, the book represents a series of talks on the key Bible texts, given over many years at 'EQUIP women', a large annual women's conference in Sydney. Some of the material on Genesis was prepared and delivered at the Katoomba Women's Convention in 2009. I am grateful to the EQUIP committee and the Katoomba Women's Convention committee for the opportunity to work so closely on this material and to share God's word with thousands of women over more than a decade. It has been a rich blessing to me, and under God's hand, I trust, to others as well. The chapter on domestic abuse is based on lectures I delivered in the 'Ministry Training for Women' course at the Presbyterian Theological Centre in Sydney.

My main aim in all that follows is to hear God's word clearly, and obey well, so that we can say with the psalmist:

> I have stored up your word in my heart,
>> that I might not sin against you…
> I will delight in your statutes;
>> I will not forget your word. (PS 119:11, 16)

1 | THE FINE DUST OF FEMINISM

O N WEDNESDAY 23 SEPTEMBER 2009, Sydney woke to a storm of red dust. For a day, the world changed. The air was thick and red. Planes were diverted. Ferries were cancelled. Traffic slowed to a crawl. Emergency departments filled with breathless casualties. Even the birds seemed mute. And while even the secular press wondered aloud if this was the end of the world, by the next day, the sky had miraculously cleared and all apocalyptic fears had been forgotten. The only reminders were hauntingly beautiful photographs, and a sepia blanket that covered every surface of the city—including every nook and cranny inside my house!

It reminded me of the impact of feminism. When feminism hit in the early 60s, the world and how we saw it changed. Some feared it was the end of the world. It was certainly the end of the world as we knew it. And there were casualties. But despite the hazards, it was intoxicating and seductively beautiful. And although the storm has now passed and the sky seems clear, the dust of feminism has reached into every part of our identity and lives. Unlike the red dust, we may not be able to see or taste it, but it is part of the cultural air we breathe.

The 'Women's Lib' movement, as it was called, swept through

Australia in my early teens. It changed beyond recognition the identity, dreams, expectations and occupations of my mother and many of her contemporaries. The tide turned against men. It was a storm of social and personal change, which was paraded and debated each night on TV, and lived out in families across the Western world. It was a bumpy ride.

You do not have to be a crack social commentator to know that since then, feminism has brought huge and radical cultural change. It is difficult to think of an element of society or our lives that has been immune from it. Everything has changed: the workforce, the family, our laws, medical practices, social etiquette, creative arts, even the games children play and the names people take. And that is just the beginning.

Feminism is now an accepted part of our society. It is unremarkable. It no longer needs to be argued as truth. It is the status quo. Those of us who might want to question some of its tenets or 'achievements' are questioning an ideology that is no longer open to question. And so our critique is dismissed as revealing more about us than about the merits of feminism.

But for those with the courage and eyes to see it, not everything feminism has brought is good, and this is nowhere more the case than in the head-on confrontation of feminism with the Christian God and with his purposes for men and women as *men* and *women*.

The dust of feminism has settled on the pages of our Bibles and obscured God's word. What the Bible once said clearly about men and women is no longer clear to us. The plain meaning of texts no longer seems plain. Some would tell us these texts mean something very different now from when they were written. Others would say that feminism has made some texts unsellable and unbelievable. In the face of these objections, and like the all-pervasive red dust, feminism has reached into every corner of Christian truth. Even God has had a feminist makeover.

But the problem is not really with God or his word.

The problem is with us. The difficulties we have with those texts that deal with the responsibilities of men and women lie in us—not in the clarity or goodness of God's word. We can expect God's word to speak clearly. And it does.

We can also expect it to mean what it says. Why would God's word say one thing and yet mean the opposite? This is, in fact, what the various 'egalitarian' interpretations do. They claim to be uncovering the true meanings of these texts, and yet their conclusions fly in the face of the words themselves. There is a gap between what the text says and what these interpretations propose it means. So for us the warning 'Mind the gap' is apt!

As in all things, our views on this matter must be based first and foremost on the actual text of Scripture. If God has chosen to speak to us in his word about his design for men and women, and he has given us his Spirit so that we might understand his word, then his word is where we must start.

To return to the dust analogy: if we want to know the true colours and contours of God's will for the roles and relationships of men and women, we must first see and study it *sans* dust!

But first, let me digress for a very brief history lesson to help us identify and understand the spread and impact of feminism.

A (really) brief history lesson

The history books tell us that feminism has had three 'waves'. The first wave came out of the intellectual movement of the 18th century called the Enlightenment, which also spawned the French and American revolutions and their respective declarations of 'the rights of man' (that is, 'people'). The key ideals were human autonomy and freedom (especially from dogma and God); the supremacy and power of human reason; and government of the people by the people and for the people.

It is little surprise then that one of the first goals of the first feminists was women's suffrage and the right to participate in democracies. In Australia, non-indigenous women have been able to vote and allowed to stand for election since Federation in 1901. It is to our shame that it took until 1962 before all our indigenous country*men* and *women* were allowed to do the same.

The second wave of feminism is what I grew up with in the 60s and 70s, when the women's lib movement was headline news. Each night on TV we saw women on university campuses burning their bras, waving placards, filling the streets in huge demonstrations, and going head to head against suited men in acrimonious public debates. My mother was a mature-aged university student at the time, and she and her friends were at the forefront of women who left the kitchen for the challenge and satisfaction of university and a career.

At its most benign, the goal was equality with men—but that often meant independence and freedom from men, and freedom from a woman's biology (possible for the first time with the new oral contraceptive pill). At the extreme end of second-wave feminism, men were to blame for the world's ills, and it was not equality with men that was sought but a reversal of order so that women would rule where men once did.

Third-wave feminism began in the early 1990s. It has many expressions and even contradictions, as do the other 'isms' currently shaping our cultural landscape (post-modernism, relativism and pluralism). For example, some third-wavers think it is empowering for women to be sex workers and pose for pornography, while others see it as the commodification of women for the pleasure of men, destroying the dignity and rights of women (I think they're right!). Significantly, third-wave theory is more about the *ambiguity* of gender and sexuality than the *rights* or *identity* of either sex, and it consciously seeks to embrace marginalized groups like women of colour, lesbians, bisexual women, women from the two-thirds world, and so on.

The good, the bad, and the ugly

Let me say up-front that I do not think feminism is to blame for everything that is wrong with the world. In fact, I do not think feminism itself is *all* bad. The gender-based inequality that feminism in its most basic form seeks to correct *is* contrary to God's purposes. So although we might not agree with the diagnosis or treatment that feminism prescribes, the symptoms or problems it identifies are often real. And feminism has brought some change for the good: women can now vote, own property, have bank accounts and an unrestricted education, and sit at board tables; rape in marriage is now a criminal offence; violence against women is now a community concern; fathers are now more involved with their children; and so on. It is a shame it was left to the feminists to force these changes, but they are good changes that sit well with God's love for justice and for all those he has made.

However, we cannot make the mistake of thinking that *only* feminism could have brought these gains. The good of feminism is entirely dependent on its reform agenda being consistent with God's reform agenda. Where it seeks to correct things that are contrary to God's good purposes—and that are due to the sin of *both* men and women—then, without intending to do so, feminism can advance God's plans for justice, peace and his glory. It has been, and can be, a tool in God's hand for advancing his good purposes.

The flipside of this is that where the agenda of feminism is *different* from God's agenda (which is most of the time), it is working against God's purposes and can bring only misery—if not in the short term then most certainly in the long term.

The other thing to remember is that society and culture are mixing pots, and feminism is not the only agent of change. There are political, economic, ideological and technological factors that all feed into each other, and it is impossible to isolate the effect of any one agent of change. So, while the rise of the 'working mother' in Western societies is undoubtedly due to feminism, it has also happened in economies with enough jobs for women to fill, and which assume and now require that households will have two incomes; and it has happened because technological advances have made it easier for women to participate in the workforce from home, and given us appliances that do with the press of a button what was once a full day's hard labour!

It should be obvious that what I have sketched here is not a detailed history or analysis of feminism or even of its effect on the church.[1] Rather, it is a broad-brushstroke picture of feminism that is both selective in what it deals with, and general in the way it deals with it. It is a shorthand introduction to one of the background 'characters' of this book.

As another background 'character' in this book, I should say that nothing surprises me more than the fact that I am its author. I am a child of my times. I was a young adult when I became a Christian, and my faith was nurtured in a tradition that valued free exercise of the gifts of the Spirit over any limitations given in the written word of God. I must have read the passages that are the focus of this book, but somehow for many years I did not notice them. My first real encounter with them was as a student at theological college in the late 80s.

Since then, the demands of life and ministry have made these Bible texts the subject of much study, which under God has produced more change in my heart and life than I ever thought possible. What is more, the more I study these texts, the more

---

1   For more detailed discussions of the history and effects of feminism and its relation to Christianity, see Kirsten Birkett, *The Essence of Feminism*, Matthias Media, Sydney, 2000; and Mary Kassian, *The Feminist Mistake*, Crossway, Wheaton, 2005.

convinced I am that *the historical understanding is right*—and the more I read the new 'egalitarian' arguments against the historical understanding, the more convinced I am that the historical understanding is right. I am not saying this journey has always been smooth sailing, but it has all been in the same direction and, I believe, propelled by the wind of the Spirit.

Given the complex and all-pervasive nature of feminism, and the huge impact it has had on us all, it is little wonder that trying to understand and accept God's purposes for men and women requires some hard work. It is like trying to read a serious book when the TV is blaring. There is just too much noise going on for us to hear clearly what God is saying—noise which is often cultural and *personal*.

To complicate things even further, sometimes this noise comes from Christian brothers and sisters who at other times have been beloved and reliable teachers and shepherds in their sermons and books. But now they tell us that these words of Scripture cannot be taken literally, or that they no longer apply today, or that the evangelistic turn-off of these texts is baggage the church cannot afford to carry and that being missional means moving with the times and fitting in with our culture.

Some of these arguments are compelling. Who among us has not been the target of jokes and jibes about the church's view on women? It would be nice to have a way out! And besides, if even the great ones cannot agree on whether and how these texts apply today, then perhaps the texts really are not clear, and the whole matter is one of wisdom and not godliness—a case of each person doing what is right in their own eyes, and giving up on ever finding *the* truth.

But when God says, "For as the heavens are higher than the earth, so are my ways higher than your ways and my thoughts than your thoughts" (Isa 55:9), he is not telling us that knowing his thoughts and ways is impossible. On the contrary, it is our privilege and task as his children to know his will and to do it.

This is why he has given us his word. Better still, he has ensured that in his written word we have all that is necessary for eternal life and faithful living (2 Pet 1:3). God's words are not just words on paper (or stone or scrolls or papyrus or whatever) but also *living* words inspired and spoken by him—and not to read on our own, but with the help of his Spirit to lead us into all truth (Heb 4:12; 2 Tim 3:16-17; John 16:13).

With such resources at our fingertips and in our hearts, our task is to sit under God's word and have it critique our culture, our lives, our relationships, our prejudices and our fears. Not vice versa. And when we do that, we find it speaks clearly and truthfully—even about the vexed issue of gender relationships, which our world has got so messed up.

This means that instead of doing what we are tempted to do— that is, assume we know what the Bible says and do our thinking with our Bibles closed—we need to go back to our Bibles, and take a closer look at these passages.

That is what this book is about. It is an opportunity to look closely at the passages that set out the nature, beauty and purpose of the relationship between men and women. And when I say 'closely', I mean text by text, verse by verse and sometimes even word by word.

The book itself falls into two parts. The first looks at those texts that deal with the roles and relationships of women and men when Christians gather together for what we call 'church'. The second section of the book focuses on their relationships within marriage, and in God's original design for creation. Each chapter is written as a discrete unit dealing with a particular text, and so can be read on its own or as part of the whole.

Perhaps studying the Bible in such a close and focused way is a new thing for you. It may even sound like hard work. I guess in some ways it is! This is no Dan Brown page-turner. That is not to say it is not exciting, but that Dan Brown page-turners are only good for a weekend—while the Bible is good for the rest of our lives, and into eternity. Also, unlike Dan Brown's books, God's word rewards our closest attention and we will never exhaust its riches.

So it is time to roll up our sleeves, open our Bibles, and pray for God's wisdom, as we turn first to consider 1 Timothy 2.

> Your hands have made and fashioned me;
> give me understanding that I may learn your
> commandments. (PS 119:73)

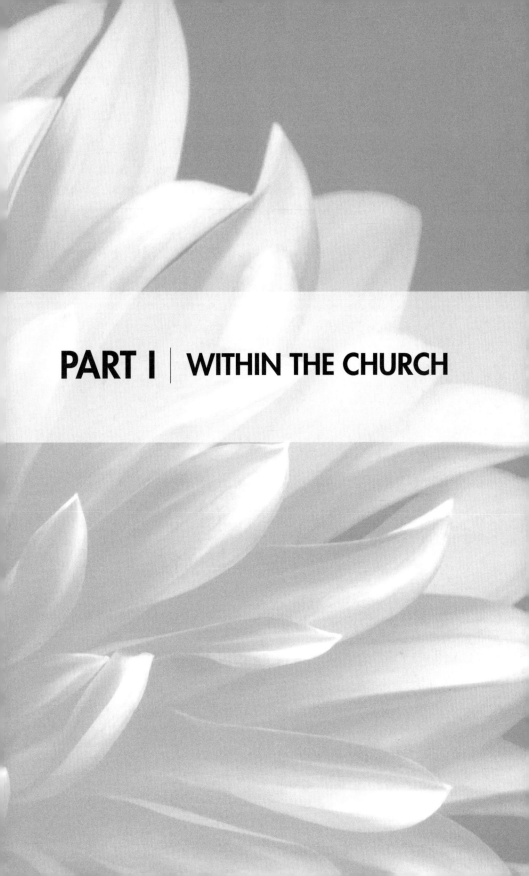

PART I | WITHIN THE CHURCH

2 | FINDING PEACE AND QUIET: 1 TIMOTHY 2

I F THE DIFFICULTY OF A PASSAGE of Scripture was decided by the heat of the debate surrounding it, or the number of books written on it, or the number of people attending seminars on it, 1 Timothy 2 must be one of the most difficult passages in the whole Bible. And given that much of the debate and most of the books concentrate on just two of the fifteen verses, we would have to conclude that these two verses must be almost impossible to understand.

And it is true that there are some conundrums in 1 Timothy 2.

When Paul says that God wants "all men to be saved" (v. 4),[1] does that exclude women? Does he really mean that Christian women should not plait their hair or wear pearls? Why does he say that Adam was not deceived but the woman was? And what about being "saved through childbearing" (v. 15)—what *was* he thinking?

These are all interesting questions and ones to which we will return, but they are not where the debate has focused. The sticking point in 1 Timothy 2 has been over two verses that (I would say)

---

1   As some Bible translations say (e.g. RSV, NIV1984, NASB, NKJV, KJ21).

are relatively uncomplicated. Those verses are:

> Let a woman learn quietly with all submissiveness. I do
> not permit a woman to teach or to exercise authority
> over a man; rather, she is to remain quiet. (vv. 11-12)

We might want to ask questions like "When?" and "Why?" and "What does 'all submissiveness' mean?" But I think if we take these verses at face value and ask the question "Can a woman teach or exercise authority over a man?" the straightforward answer would have to be "No".

This was illustrated to me a few years back by a friend who is a pastor in an ethnic-based church. He had been meeting to read the Bible with a university-aged woman who was a new Christian, and they were reading Paul's first letter to Timothy. They got to chapter 2 and read it, and he waited for the protests he was used to hearing about these two verses.

There was a lull. Silence. "Do you have any questions?" my friend asked.

"No, it's self-explanatory", the woman replied.

"Do you have any problems with what Paul's saying?" he asked.

"No", she replied. "It's easy. Paul is saying women shouldn't teach in church, because that's the way God wants it."

Granted, this is just one woman's experience. But this was a new Christian meeting a passage that most women (and many men) these days baulk at, and understanding it and accepting it at face value.

Now we might say, "Oh well, her ethnic cultural background probably made it easier for her to do that", and that may be true. But can you see that the opposite might also be true—that *our* culture influences *our* reading of the text, and that many of the difficulties we find in it might exist because of *our* culture and *our* personalities and not because of the text itself?

We do not have to answer these questions now, but at the very least we need to be aware that we do not come to the text as neutral readers. We all have cultural blind spots and sensitivities that influence our reading. There is no way we can avoid that.

What we *can* avoid is being unaware and uncritical of our own personal and cultural 'glasses'. The Bible was written, and has always been read, by people living in real-time cultures. Yet, God promises that his Spirit-breathed word continues to speak his truth clearly, and that his Spirit, whom he has given us, will lead us into all truth (John 16:13; 2 Tim 3:16). This means that we must always allow God's word to critique us and our culture, rather than the other way around.

With that word of caution, let us turn to 1 Timothy 2.

Plain reading

> ¹First of all, then, I urge that supplications, prayers, intercessions, and thanksgivings be made for all people, ²for kings and all who are in high positions, that we may lead a peaceful and quiet life, godly and dignified in every way. ³This is good, and it is pleasing in the sight of God our Saviour, ⁴who desires all people to be saved and to come to the knowledge of the truth. ⁵For there is one God, and there is one mediator between God and men, the man Christ Jesus, ⁶who gave himself as a ransom for all, which is the testimony given at the proper time. ⁷For this I was appointed a preacher and an apostle (I am telling the truth, I am not lying), a teacher of the Gentiles in faith and truth.
>
> ⁸I desire then that in every place the men should pray, lifting holy hands without anger or quarrelling; ⁹likewise also that women should adorn themselves in respectable apparel, with modesty and self-control, not

with braided hair and gold or pearls or costly attire, [10]but with what is proper for women who profess godliness—with good works. [11]Let a woman learn quietly with all submissiveness. [12]I do not permit a woman to teach or to exercise authority over a man; rather, she is to remain quiet. [13] For Adam was formed first, then Eve; [14] and Adam was not deceived, but the woman was deceived and became a transgressor. [15]Yet she will be saved through childbearing—if they continue in faith and love and holiness, with self-control. (1 TIMOTHY 2)

The first thing we notice is that the chapter begins with a 'then'.[2] This lets us know that what follows is actually dependent on what went before, where Paul charged Timothy with the duty of resisting false teaching (1:3-7, 18-20), and also spelt out the wonderful gospel of God's grace for sinners, amongst whom Paul was the foremost (1:12-17).

So it is in light of this gospel, and the need to defend it, that Paul urges Timothy and the Ephesian believers to make it their priority to make "supplications, prayers, intercessions, and thanksgivings" for all people, particularly kings and all those in authority (2:1-2). In every way possible, Paul urges, pray—pray for those you know and those you do not, especially those in high places.

And why are they to pray like this?

First, they are to pray because social stability is a blessing. As the gospel filters upwards in society to those in positions of power, the benefit of a stable and just society filters downward and everyone benefits. A society permeated by the gospel is a better society for everyone. And for Christians it frees us to get on with godly, quiet Christian living (v. 2).

---

2   Some translations have 'therefore' here and/or in verse 8.

But the second reason they are to pray is that such prayers are good and pleasing to God our Saviour, because he wants all people to be saved (vv. 3-4). Paul does not specify the content of the prayers to be prayed, but this is their ultimate goal. God longs for all to be saved, and for his people to join in that task in and through prayer. Indeed, prayer for the salvation of all people is prayer reflecting the very heart of God. What a privilege that we can do it!

Paul then gives us the reason for this universal scope of salvation. It is that God is one (v. 5). The nature of God himself is the reason for the universal application of the gospel. There is only one Saviour God, and only one mediator Jesus Christ, and only one ransom paid by him for all people.

There is not one god for Jews and another for Gentiles, or one saviour for the lowly and another for kings. There is one Saviour, one mediator, and one ransom—sufficient for all types of people and available to all.

Which is why Paul then moves to his apostleship (v. 7)— because his own cross-cultural ministry as a Jew evangelizing the Gentiles is motivated by, and is a demonstration of, the universal scope of the gospel. This one God has one gospel, and it is not captive to social boundaries (Gal 3:28).

'Therefore', Paul writes, 'as a consequence of this boundary-jumping salvation mission of God, I want men in every place to pray' (1 Tim 2:8). If his first charge to prayer has not tipped us off that his comments are aimed at what Christians are to do together when they meet, the phrase "in every place" makes it clear. Paul uses this phrase elsewhere to refer to the geographical spread of Christian communities (1 Cor 1:2; 2 Cor 2:14; 1 Thess 1:8).[3] It may also reflect Malachi 1:11, which links the wide geographical spread of places of worship with the inclusion of the Gentiles

---

3   The same phrase is used each time in the original Greek.

in God's covenant—which we have just been told is Paul's own mission, and God's desire.

This means that although Paul probably had the house churches of the city of Ephesus at the front of his mind when he wrote the letter of 1 Timothy, its relevance does not end there. His whole purpose in writing was so that these Christians would know how to conduct themselves as the "household of God" (3:14-15)— and he knew *that* household extended geographically, culturally, and temporally far beyond Ephesus.

However, Paul does not just want prayer being offered from every place; he also wants prayer that is holy and "without anger or quarrelling" (2:8).

What is important is not just *that* prayer is offered, and that it is offered from every place Christians meet, but also that the *manner* in which it is offered is consonant with the gospel.

Those who are praying are to lift their hands in sincere and urgent prayer for all people, and they are to be at peace with God and with each other. What can strike us in our context is the lifting of their hands, but there is nothing particularly remarkable about this as it was the usual posture for prayer. Rather, it is the emphasis of Paul's command that should strike us: the 'holiness' that is to characterize the praying—holiness seen in the absence of anger and quarrelling. Now, whether or not this instruction was responding to a live problem in Ephesus, there is a universally valid principle here: male aggression and self-promotion are not to hinder holy prayer.

Paul then addresses the women (vv. 9-15). Their issue is not anger management; it is their presentation—their conduct and demeanour. Paul tells them to dress modestly. Their appearance is not to be gauche, sexually provocative, brash or showy, and neither is their manner. Their behaviour, like their dress, is to show restraint and modesty, good judgement and self-control.

They are also to be proactive in doing good. What is to draw attention to them is not how they look but how they live, and there is to be a visual correlation between their talk and their walk. Their lives are to reflect the fact that they worship God. Female vanity and self-promotion are not to hinder holiness.

Which brings us to the verses that have been the focus of so much attention (vv. 11-12). Much can be (and has been) said about the various ways of understanding and applying these 29 words—just 19 in the original Greek—but for now we will just do an exercise in comprehension.

Verse 11 opens: "Let a woman learn" (which I take it is pretty straightforward). How is she to learn? She is to learn "quietly with all submissiveness". At the very least, this tells us that women are to be part of the learning process that Paul alluded to earlier (v. 4).

Women are to come to the knowledge of the truth of the gospel—but they are to come to that knowledge in a certain way. They are not to challenge or dispute what is taught. They are to have minds willing to learn and hearts ready to obey. Their manner of learning, as with their manner of dress and conduct generally, is to display a quiet decorum.

And following this instruction about what women *are* to do when teaching occurs is instruction about what they are *not* to do. They are to learn, Paul says, but they are not "to teach or to exercise authority over a man" (v. 12).

I will say more on this later, but at face value these verses are saying that learning and teaching are two different activities. One is okay for women to do; the other is not (at least not in the situation Paul is addressing—the public community gathering). These verses are also saying (again, at face value) that when it comes to teaching the gathered Christian community, women are to keep quiet. They are not to teach. Teaching is someone else's responsibility, not theirs.

Significantly, Paul is not saying that women are not competent to teach, or that they may never teach. Elsewhere he encourages women to teach other women and children (Titus 2:3-5; Eph 6:1; cf. 1 Tim 5:9-10), and commends the instruction a church leader received from his mother and grandmother (2 Tim 1:5, 3:14-15). He urges *all* believers to teach and encourage one another as they sing together (Col 3:16). Women also contribute to the Christian assembly in activities with the potential to teach, such as prophecy and prayer (1 Cor 11:4-5; 14:3-5, 12-19, 24-26, 31).[4]

But these activities are not what is on view in 1 Timothy 2. What is on view is a certain sort of teaching in the Christian community gathering that women are not to do.

Now many people today say that these two verses are incredibly obscure and difficult to understand. But at a simple comprehension level I do not believe that is true.

Several years ago in the midst of a debate about the ordination of women, a young non-Christian reporter asked me if there was a verse in the Bible to support my belief that women ought not to be ordained as congregational leaders. I quoted her these two verses from 1 Timothy 2. She wrote them down and read them back to me.

"That's what it says?" she asked me, looking puzzled.

"Yes, that's what it says", I replied, preparing myself to explain what it meant and why it applied to today's church and why it meant that women ought not be ordained.

But there was no need, because her response was, "Well, what's the argument about then? I would've thought if that's what it says, that settles it. Doesn't it?"

Interestingly, when the story appeared that night on the

---

4   The Greek word translated as 'brothers' in 14:26 can also mean 'brothers and sisters', as the ESV notes elsewhere: "Or *brothers and sisters*. The plural Greek word *adelphoi* (translated 'brothers') refers to siblings in a family. In New Testament usage, depending on the context, *adelphoi* may refer either to men or to both men and women who are siblings (brothers and sisters) in God's family, the church."

TV news, the two verses were printed out on the screen so that everyone could read them. Clearly, this reporter thought they were pretty self-explanatory!

So let us move on to see the reasons Paul gives for his command.

He takes us back to the first few chapters of the Bible, to the accounts of the creation and fall of humanity, and from there he gives us two reasons. First, that "Adam was formed first, then Eve" (v. 13); and second, that "Adam was not deceived, but the woman was deceived and became a transgressor [or sinner]" (v. 14).

When we turn to Genesis 2 we find that Paul is right. The man was formed first and the woman second (Gen 2:21-22).

And again, although we may have missed it in our reading of Genesis 3, it does say that Eve was deceived. When the Lord God asks her "What is this that you have done?" Eve replies, "The serpent deceived me, and I ate" (v. 13). Interestingly, Genesis does not say that Adam was deceived. He sinned—yes—but it does not say he was deceived.

Paul is not pulling exegetical rabbits out of hats. He is not saying Genesis says anything more than what it actually says, though perhaps he is drawing out implications that we may not have expected.

So our comprehension exercise has shown that women are given two instructions—one about something they are to do (i.e. learn quietly and with all submissiveness), and one about things they are not to do (i.e. teach or exercise authority over men)—and two reasons for those instructions, both drawn from Adam and Eve.

Which brings us to the last verse in this chapter, and perhaps the trickiest of them all—so tricky that even the various Bible translations cannot agree how the verse should read. I think the best translation is the one given by the ESV, but drawing out the contrast with the previous verses: "*But* she will be saved through childbearing—if they continue in faith and love and holiness, with self-control" (1 Tim 2:15).

What started out as an encouragement to pray, and moved to gender appropriate behaviour in the Christian assembly, ends with this enigmatic verse. What does it mean that *she* will be saved through childbearing if *they* continue in faith, love and holiness with self-control? And saved from what? And how is this a conclusion to Paul's instructions?

For the time being, hold those thoughts!

Questions arising from plain reading

First we need to go through the text and answer some of the questions arising from the exercise in comprehension we have just completed.

1. God wants all men to be saved

For many of us sensitive to gendered language, our first stumbling block is that many translations read that God "wants all *men* to be saved" (v. 4).[5] This problem is repeated in the next verse, which similarly says "there is one God, and there is one mediator between God and *men*, the man Christ Jesus" (v. 5).[6] "What about the women?" I hear you ask. "Are they left out?"

Well, the answer is "No! Of course they're not left out!"

In fact, one of the interesting features of 1 Timothy 2 is the words Paul uses for 'man' and 'woman'. At the beginning of the chapter, when he is focusing on the universal scope of salvation and the one mediator between God and humanity, the word in the original language (Greek) is the generic term for 'man' (*anthrōpos*). When he comes to talk more directly to men and then to women in the second half of the chapter, he changes to the gender-specific terms.

In verse 5 then, where salvation is on view, Paul deliberately

5   RSV, NIV1984, NASB, NKJV, KJ21
6   ESV, RSV, NIV1984, NASB, NKJV, KJ21

uses the more inclusive generic term because he is talking about what all people have in common: the need for a saviour arising from our common state of sinfulness (cf. 1:15-16). And when Paul describes this saviour as "the *man* Christ Jesus" it packs an even greater punch, because the word he uses is not the gender-specific 'man' (*anēr*)—which he could have used, and which he will go on to use when he addresses the men (2:8)—but the general word 'man' (*anthrōpos*) as representative 'man' for all humankind: for both women and men.

So in actual fact what might have struck us as language excluding women is actually rich, inclusive language, where Paul is highlighting Jesus' shared human identity with us all, and God's desire that all women and men will be saved.

2. All submissiveness

The next thing that strikes many of us as in need of explanation is when Paul says a woman should learn "with all submissiveness" (v. 11). What does 'submissiveness' mean here? Again, taking a look at the original language will help us.

The word that Paul uses here and a related verb meaning 'submit' are used often in the New Testament, and in the context of many different types of relationships. Children are to submit to their parents (Luke 2:51; 1 Tim 3:4; cf. Titus 1:6). Slaves are to submit to their masters (Titus 2:9; 1 Pet 2:18-25). Wives are to submit themselves to their husbands (1 Cor 14:34-35; Eph 5:24; Col 3:18; Titus 2:5; 1 Pet 3:1, 5).[7] Christians are to submit to those over them in Christian leadership (1 Cor 16:15-16; 1 Pet 5:5).[8] We are to submit ourselves to God (Jas 4:7), and as part of that God-ward submission, we are to submit to governing authorities (Rom 13:1; Titus 3:1; 1 Pet 2:13). However, this language of

---

7 We will examine two of these in later chapters.
8 cf. Hebrews 13:17, where the language is different but the idea is the same.

submission is not limited to human relationships. All things have been subjected and will ultimately submit to Christ (Eph 1:22; Phil 3:21; Heb 2:5, 8; 1 Pet 3:22). Demons submit to the rule of Christ (Luke 10:17). The church is to submit to Christ as her head (Eph 5:24). And when all things have been made subject to him, Christ himself will submit to God the Father (1 Cor 15:27-28).

Obviously we will revisit this idea of submission several times in this book, and each return visit will fill out the picture more. But this quick survey of the New Testament allows us to say with absolute certainty that submission is a common Christian response. In fact, it is fundamental to the life of faith. This quick overview also allows us to say that except for those instances where it refers to the judging rule of Christ, submission is a voluntary and willing acceptance of the leadership and responsibility of another.

But in 1 Timothy 2, to whom are women to be submissive? To God? To sound teaching? To the teachers?

In the original language, verses 11-12 form a carefully balanced unit and run in parallel to each other. The words 'in quietness' appear at the beginning of verse 11 and the end of verse 12, like bookends, underlining the main point about the conduct of women—a point that has already been made about the quiet, godly life Christians are to lead (v. 2). Also, the two things commanded in verse 11—"learn" and "all submissiveness"—pair up and contrast with the two prohibited activities in verse 12—"teach" and "exercise authority over a man", respectively.[9]

This helps to answer our question. The circumstances of their learning, and the prohibition against having authority over men, point us to the details of their submissiveness.

---

[9]

2:11	in quietness		
		learn	with all submissiveness
2:12		(not) to teach	(not) to exercise authority over men
			in quietness

The setting for the women's learning is the Christian gathering—the same setting as for the praying Paul has just commanded. The women are to learn quietly rather than to teach. And instead of having "authority over a man" they are to do their learning "with all submissiveness".

Since not all men have responsibility to teach and lead the congregation (as we would find if we read on in chapter 3), Paul is not saying that all women are to submit themselves to all men, all the time. Rather, women are to be submissive *in* church, *when* the teaching is happening, *to* what is taught and those men who are teaching it.

In practice, this means that women are not to be authoritative teachers of the gathered household of God. Instead, they are to learn from those men who labour in preaching (3:2, 5:17), and they are to learn with quiet, willing and voluntary submissiveness, accepting what is taught and the authority of those teaching it. Their responsibility is to learn quietly and submissively—conduct that is fitting for women who profess godliness.

3. Adam and Eve

Which brings us to Adam and Eve, from whom Paul draws his two reasons for restricting women from the authoritative teaching role. Why does he refer to Adam and Eve?

Paul goes right back to the Genesis accounts because it was then that God's intentions for men and women were first enunciated and then violated. These foundational chapters of Genesis will occupy us in a later chapter, but for now we will pick up on the two aspects on which Paul focuses our attention here.

Genesis 2 tells us that God formed the man first and placed him in the garden to tend it. Creation to this point had been totally good. The refrain "And God saw that it was good" runs through Genesis 1 and 2 until Genesis 2:18, when the Lord God said, "It is not good that the man should be alone; I will make him a helper fit for him".

This helper, as we know, was the woman—flesh of his flesh, bone of his bone. Both man and woman were *equally* made in the image of God, as Genesis 1 tells us; both were given the divine mandate to "fill the earth and subdue it" (v. 28). They were made of the same stuff but given different responsibilities. He was the firstborn; she was the helper.

That is Paul's point when he says, "Adam was formed first, then Eve" (1 Tim 2:13). The man in Genesis 2 clearly had temporal priority to the woman. He was made first. And so he is the firstborn, with the responsibilities that go with that, whereas she was formed after him, to accompany him and help in fulfilling their common mandate.

The first reason Paul gives for his instructions to women is based on the way things are meant to be; the way God originally created men and women.

The second reason, however, is based on what happened when God's ideal was disobeyed (1 Tim 2:14). Eve, as we know, took it upon herself to doubt God's word, and followed the serpent's advice and ate the fruit. She gave some to the man who was with her, and he ate too (Gen 3:1-7).

They both sinned at that point. But Genesis 3 makes it clear that they sinned in different ways. Instead of trusting the truthfulness and goodness of God's word, Eve was deceived by the serpent and led into sin, and after she ate she also led her husband into sin. Adam, on the other hand, had been given the responsibility to lead his wife—not listen to her and follow her into sin. He disobeyed God by eating the fruit God had told him not to eat (2:17), and by abdicating his responsibility of leadership to his wife (3:17).

Paul refers to these two episodes from Genesis because the principles of God's creation have not changed. This pattern of relationships, he is saying, transcends time and culture. We might say it is 'transcultural'. What was ideal in the garden still applies.

The pattern of male leadership and female submission that

God first established is to be the pattern for the Ephesian church. And the disruption of that pattern seen in the Fall is not to be repeated. The women are not to usurp the male leadership God has provided. Instead they are to accept willingly the God-given differences in gender responsibilities. They are to accept male leadership and express that in their attitude to learning and by not teaching or having authority over men.

And I take it that Christian women today are to do the same.

This is not because women are less intelligent, less gifted, less useful, more gullible or somehow inferior. They are not—and these are not the reasons given for the commands. Paul says nothing here about women's capabilities, and it is clear elsewhere that he recognizes the valuable and God-given gifting and contribution of women in the progress of the gospel and the life of the church.

Nevertheless, because of God's creation purposes for men and women, and because of the events of the Fall, the participation and contribution of women in the Christian assembly is to be different from those of men—and in this text, most particularly those men God has gifted and appointed to teach and lead our local Christian communities.

The battle for women in our day is to accept God's wisdom in this and be content with it, when our entire culture has taught us not to be. The battle for men, as it was in Genesis 3, is to step up to the sort of leadership Paul has in mind, when our entire culture insists that women are the real 'go-to' men, and that men and boys have little to contribute beyond being the butt of jokes.

4. Saved through childbearing

This brings us to the last verse of 1 Timothy 2, which presents so many conundrums that the major Bible translations cannot even agree how it should be translated. My preference is a slight variation on the ESV translation: "*But* she will be saved through childbearing—if they continue in faith and love and holiness, with self-control" (v. 15).

What does Paul mean when he says the woman will be saved through childbearing? Here is a selection of how this has been understood.

Some people have suggested it means that Christian women will be kept safe in childbirth, or that they will be spared the pain of childbirth that resulted from the Fall (Gen 3:16). You will quickly realize there are many problems with these views, not the least of which is that experience does not bear them out. Sadly, godly women have died in childbirth, and pain-free, drug-free labour this side of Eden is an oxymoron.

More than this, however, the word used here in 1 Timothy 2 and translated as either 'kept safe' or 'saved' is the word that Paul consistently used in his letters for 'saved'. And he uses this word to refer not to *physical* wellbeing but to *spiritual* salvation from sin and judgement.

But does that mean Paul is advocating salvation by works (i.e. childbearing) and not by faith alone? No—he has already said that salvation is by faith (cf. 1:4, 16; 2:7; it even gets a mention here in 2:15).

So if Paul is not referring to *physical* wellbeing and is not advocating salvation *by works*, what is he saying?

Broadly speaking, there are two more options. Both have things going for them, but I prefer the second.

Some people suggest that "childbearing" is actually a reference to Christ, picking up on the promise of Genesis 3:15 where the seed of the woman will "bruise" the serpent's head. 1 Timothy 2:15 then means that even though she was deceived and became a sinner, Eve will be saved through the birth of Christ, since he defeated Satan and made salvation possible. And like Eve, women generally will be saved if they continue to live lives of faith and love and holiness, with self-control.

This has the benefit of explaining the link with Eve in the previous verse and explains the movement from "she" to "they" in this verse, as it has a particular woman and particular childbirth in mind. But if Paul meant the birth of Christ, he picked an uncharacteristically obtuse way of saying it—especially when there is a better solution.

When we look closely at the whole letter, we find that this verse bears several similarities to Paul's later instruction to Timothy that he is to watch his life and teaching closely, and to "persist" in this, because by doing so he will "save" himself and his hearers (4:16). Timothy, of course, would not actually save his hearers—Paul is quite clear that only Jesus can do that—but by faithfully discharging his responsibilities of godly living and true teaching, Timothy would ensure that neither he nor those in his charge would depart from the truth and shipwreck their faith. Their faith would be preserved from (or would escape) the very real spiritual dangers besetting it.

This helps us to understand what Paul means in reference to women. It helps us to see that he is not talking about childbirth being a *means* of salvation, but about Christian women being spiritually preserved or saved from the temptations and fate of Eve and the dangers of false teaching, if they continue in faith and love and holiness with self-control. And childbearing is part of that.

Childbearing is one of the good works with which godly women are to adorn themselves, even though its goodness and godliness appears to have been under threat (cf. 4:3, 5:14-15). It seems to function as a shorthand way of referring to responsibilities that were peculiar to women.

Even in our feminist culture (Arnold Schwarzenegger's efforts in *Junior* notwithstanding), men do not and cannot have babies. Childbearing remains the most distinctive difference in the responsibilities of men and women. It is a peculiarly female responsibility—it was in the garden of Eden, it was in the first century, and it is now—and so it can function here as a shorthand for those differences.

Viewed this way, 2:15 assures Christian women that their faith will be kept safe if they embrace their particular God-given female responsibilities. Instead of leaving their roles and assuming the male responsibilities of teaching and leadership—thinking, as Eve did, that this would make them more 'spiritual'—these Christian women will avoid her error and her fate.[10] They will be preserved—in much the same way that Timothy and his hearers will be saved by him faithfully fulfilling his God-given responsibilities.

This does not mean that all Christian women must have children; rather, that women are to be content with the roles and responsibilities God has ordained for them. That might include children; it might not. It might include marriage; it might not. But however their lives unfold, women are to be content with the patterns of relationship between men and women that God has instituted for our own good.

Whether or not you are convinced by this explanation, it is important to realize that verse 15 does not affect the substance of the passage in terms of women teaching or having authority over men. Whatever we decide about this verse, the rest still stands.

Why the plain reading is rejected

Now it is time look briefly at the arguments used to reject the substance of this passage.

One of the things I like about winter is Rugby Union. I love watching it on TV, especially when the Australian Wallabies play the New Zealand All Blacks. At those games, when the cameras

---

10 See AJ Köstenberger, 'Ascertaining Women's God-Ordained Roles: An Interpretation of 1 Timothy 2:15', *Bulletin for Biblical Research*, 7, 1997, pp. 107-44.

pan over the crowds, you can see at a glance which team each person is barracking for. There are only two types of supporters: those wearing and waving the Australian green and gold, and the New Zealanders doing the same in black.

It is easy to think the debate about 1 Timothy 2 similarly falls into two sharply defined camps: those who accept and apply this passage today and those who do not. But that's not actually how it is.

Sure, there are two groups of opinion: one that says these verses mean what they say and should be practised in our churches, and another that believes otherwise. But that is where the agreement amongst this second group ends. You see, whilst they agree the verses no longer apply, there is no agreement as to *why* that is so. Their theories even cancel out and contradict each other. It is as though their team has a group of players all working hard to beat each other!

Because of this, there is a myriad of different views. We will look briefly at the main ones, moving from views that find little sympathy amongst people who take the Bible seriously to views we might have encountered in our own churches or from friends and family.

1. Not God's word

The first two 'extreme' objections are ones that assume either that Paul did not write 1 Timothy or that Paul was wrong in what he wrote. In these views, the verses do not apply and cannot be taken seriously because the instruction does not come with apostolic authority—either because it was not written by Paul, or because it was written by him but he was wrong in what he wrote. These verses are therefore an aberration rather than the mind of God.

The question of the authorship of the Pastoral Epistles[11] has had much ink spent on it. But at the end of the day, 1 Timothy

---

11 This is a common collective name for the three letters we know as 1 and 2 Timothy and Titus.

claims to have been written by the apostle, was accepted in the early church as having been written by the apostle, and bears all the marks of having been written by the apostle (in terms of its themes and teaching). And we know from Acts and several of Paul's letters that he worked closely with Timothy and had a deep affection for him (1 Cor 4:17; 2 Cor 1:19; 1 Thess 3:6).

Some people point out differences in vocabulary between the Pastoral Epistles and some of Paul's other letters. However, these variations can easily be explained by the personal nature of these three short letters and the somewhat later date at which they were written—besides which, scholars tell us we all change our vocabulary depending on what is being discussed (which is hardly rocket science when you think about it!).

So I believe we can confidently say that Paul wrote this letter, and that it comes to us with his apostolic authority and is reliably the word of God.

2. God's word but...

But does it apply today? I have argued that it does, however some who call themselves evangelicals say it does not.

A common thread in such arguments is the use of Galatians 3:28 to cancel out 1 Timothy 2. It is as if only one text can be right, and Galatians wins the day. Galatians 3:28 says, "There is neither Jew nor Greek, there is neither slave nor free, there is no male and female, for you are all one in Christ Jesus". Those who use this passage say that what is required of women in 1 Timothy 2 contravenes the equality between the sexes in Galatians 3:28, which they argue says the gospel eradicates the differences between men and women and so there should be no restrictions on women's ministry.

But we cannot use one passage of the Bible to cancel out another—especially when the sentiment of 1 Timothy 2 is reflected in other passages on the relationships of men and women in church and marriage, and for similar reasons (i.e. 1 Cor 11:3-16, 14:33b-35; Eph 5:21-33; Col 3:18-19; Titus 2:3-5; 1 Pet 3:1-7). It is not an either/or decision between Galatians 3:28 and these other texts. They all need to be understood in context and then held in balance—not used to cancel each other out.

If a church in its application of 1 Timothy 2:11-12 prevented women from participating at all in the public meeting, or said the salvation women are granted is something less than that given to men, then they would be as much in error as those people and churches that want to sideline 1 Timothy 2 on the basis of Galatians 3. Both 1 Timothy 2 and our equality in Christ can and must be adhered to simultaneously.

But the fact is that Galatians 3:28 is not talking about the ministry of women or about the roles of women and men. It is talking about the unity that salvation in Christ brings to otherwise disparate groups of people. People who were previously at odds are brought together in the gospel. There is now no division in Christ Jesus. Our salvation brings us together in him and makes us heirs of the same promise and adopted children of the same God. We can see this clearly when we read the verse in its broader context:

> Know then that it is those of faith who are the sons
> of Abraham. And the Scripture, foreseeing that God
> would justify the Gentiles by faith, preached the gospel
> beforehand to Abraham, saying, "In you shall all the
> nations be blessed." So then, those who are of faith are
> blessed along with Abraham, the man of faith...
>
> So then, the law was our guardian until Christ came,
> in order that we might be justified by faith. But now that
> faith has come, we are no longer under a guardian, for in
> Christ Jesus you are all sons of God, through faith. For
> as many of you as were baptized into Christ have put on

Christ. There is neither Jew nor Greek, there is neither slave nor free, there is no male and female, for you are all one in Christ Jesus. And if you are Christ's, then you are Abraham's offspring, heirs according to promise.

(GAL 3:7-9, 24-29)

Galatians 3:28 is a wonderful verse about our full acceptance, unity and common experience in Christ, but it does not bring male and female differences to an end. These differences continue, and are to be reflected in our fellowship together—as other parts of God's word make clear.

All the same, we need to look briefly at the various ways in which Galatians 3 is used to argue against the application of 1 Timothy 2 to today's church.

The first of these might be described as the 'just Ephesus' or 'just certain women' argument. It maintains that Paul's instructions are *ad hoc* in nature. That is, Paul was responding to specific problems in the Ephesian church at that time—either of false teaching or certain women causing trouble within the congregation. Since these instructions were written for those specific circumstances then they applied *only* in those circumstances. They were the right instructions then, but only then. They are the wrong instructions now. Instead, Galatians 3:28 provides the paradigm for the way things should be now.

However, while it is true that Paul's instructions appear to have been written to correct an actual problem in an actual church, we cannot dismiss them so quickly. Why would Paul use heavy theological artillery drawn from Genesis if the problem was really just a local aberration that needed a firm apostolic hand?

The fact that Paul uses arguments drawn from Adam and Eve tells us that the principles informing his instructions transcend culture, because he is pointing to God's pattern of relationships established at creation, rejected in the Fall, and restored in Christ.

And so it remains relevant for us. The precise application may change in different cultures, but the principle remains the same.

Furthermore, what is to say that the proposed reconstructions of the problems in the city of Ephesus or in the Ephesian congregation are correct? Even those who propose this *ad hoc* solution cannot agree on what problem the church faced. And even if one of them is correct, what is to say that the same problem does not exist today?

In short, Paul's instructions may have been written to correct a particular situation, but they contain teaching that is relevant far beyond that immediate situation.

Another argument limiting the application of 1 Timothy 2 says that the problem is not women teaching men—it is just the *way* they were doing it. So one view says it is okay for women to teach as long as they do not do it in a bossy way. Another view says it is okay for women to teach in church, so long as they do it under the authority of the male minister/pastor.

The main problem with these views is that it is not what the apostle Paul *says*. He says that a woman is *not permitted to teach men*—not that she *is* permitted to teach *provided* she does it in a certain way. The text says that a woman is not to teach men, and the teaching on view in this passage (as in the rest of the Pastoral Epistles) is the ongoing, authoritative and public exposition of God's truth (cf. 2:7; 4:11, 13, 16; 5:17; 6:2c-3). It is what we call 'the sermon', the public authoritative proclamation of God's truth. The activity is what we call 'preaching'.

In addition to this main problem, the first view rests on a very dubious (and widely discredited) translation of the Greek word for "exercise authority over" (*authenteō*), and the second view assumes that 'teaching' and 'having authority' are two completely different activities with no overlap. They are indeed distinct activities, but they are not mutually exclusive. This type of teaching *does* have authority as it is the ongoing formal instruction of the

Christian community, and the pastoral and relational authority on view is exercised in part through teaching (3:2, 4:11, 5:17, 6:2c). It is also worth noting that the type of speech that happens under the authority of other people in the New Testament is not preaching or teaching, but *prophecy*—as we will see when we get to 1 Corinthians 11 and 14.

Whichever way we cut it, 1 Timothy 2 prevents women from teaching or having authority over men in the Christian gathering; it does not merely prevent them from doing it *in a certain way*.

Another line of argument says that Paul wrote these commands as an accommodation to the prevailing culture, but that the right relationship between men and women is seen in Galatians 3:28. Paul did not want to upset social convention, this view says, so he was happy for early Christians to maintain the *status quo* and not rock the cultural boat. But when those conventions cease to be an obstacle, the differences between men and women are to be removed à la (the alleged meaning of) Galatians 3:28.

Against this view, we need to notice again Paul's use of Adam and Eve as the reason for his instructions. From Genesis we can see that male leadership and female submission are not a result of the Fall, and they are not reversed in Christ. Rather, this pattern of relationships *predates* the Fall and represents God's perfect intentions for humanity.

Besides all this, Paul was more than happy to challenge social conventions when they contradicted the gospel and God's truth and justice (as was Jesus), so this theory of cultural accommodation fails for yet another reason.

Another argument claims that the New Testament depicts women teaching, so Paul's rules about women teaching did not even apply in the early church. And, as we have seen, women did teach. Eunice and Lois taught Timothy (2 Tim 1:5). Priscilla, along with her husband Aquila, instructed Apollos (Acts 18:26). Older women were to teach younger women (Titus 2:3-5). Women could also sing and pray and prophesy, all of which could teach (Col 3:16; 1 Cor 11:4-5; 14:3-5, 12-19, 24, 26, 31).

But none of these examples are women teaching men in the authoritative instruction that happened when the Christian community assembled. Even Paul's mention of Euodia and Syntyche (Phil 4:2-3) and Junia (Rom 16:7)[12]—who *may* have been involved in some sort of gospel proclamation—does not indicate that they taught men, so to claim these women had a public teaching role to men within the church gathering requires several leaps of logic and an argument from silence. It is just not on.

But what about the argument that 1 Corinthians 11 allows women to prophesy, and that preaching is akin to prophecy?

Again, this argument fails. It is true: there are similarities between preaching and prophecy. Both are verbal, and both are done within the congregation. But they are clearly different too. Paul distinguishes between them (Rom 12:6-7; 1 Cor 12:28-29; Eph 4:11). He also allows women to do one and forbids them to do the other. One must be evaluated to see if it is to be accepted; the other is authoritative. If a prophecy is weighed and found wanting then the speaker suffers no harm, but false teachers are to be expelled from the congregation.

Whatever they have in common, prophecy and preaching are clearly not the same thing. So once again, this is not a reason to dispense with Paul's prohibition against women teaching and having authority over men.

Still another argument claims that the restrictions in 1 Timothy 2:12 only apply to married women. But again this does not work.

---

12   It is not clear whether this name refers to a man or a woman. But even if it is a woman, and even if we accept the NIV (she was "outstanding among the apostles") rather than the ESV (she was "well known to the apostles")—although the ESV translation is more likely—Paul does not say her ministry was identical to that of the male apostles.

Whilst the original word for 'woman' is the same as that for 'wife' (*gunē*), and 'man' is the same word as 'husband' (*anēr*), the context gives us enough clues to know that it is women and men generally whom Paul is addressing, not just those who are married. The setting is the church not the home, and while Adam and Eve were husband and wife, they are also representative of us all. Moreover, it would be a stretch to suggest that Paul wants only married men to pray with holiness and without anger and quarrelling, or only married women to be modest and known for their good works and not their flashy attire.

We must conclude that Paul's instructions are intended for us all.

There is one last argument to consider in this long list of 'God's word but…' objections. There are some who would agree that these verses are God's word, and that they restrict women from engaging in the formal, ongoing, authoritative teaching of the church. But, the argument goes, now that the Bible is written and we all have access to it, this sort of teaching activity is no longer done—by anyone, not even men.

Obviously there are some differences between the first century and today when it comes to the Bible, and I suspect we often take for granted the immense privilege of reading and studying all of God's inspired word whenever we want. But as I see it, there are two main problems with this view.

The first is that it uses the historical fact of the production and publication of the New Testament to silence the text of the New Testament. We can be confident that God's sovereign and providential hand guided the collection and acceptance of the books. And we should be grateful for the invention of the printing press, which has made the task of copying Scripture so much easier. But there is no hint anywhere in God's word, Old Testament or New, that the creation of 'the Bible' would render bits of 'the Bible' wrong or obsolete. And this silence alone should caution us.

The second problem with this view is that it makes too much of a distinction between the New Testament era and our own situation. Even within the New Testament it is clear that the early Christians had authoritative writings. There was the 'Jewish Scripture', or Old Testament, which was the written word of God and which permeates the New Testament to such an extent that we must assume it was widely known (2 Tim 3:15-16; 1 Cor 10:11).[13] There were the apostles' letters, which were to be read aloud, preserved and passed on, and which provided the basis for ongoing Christian instruction (1 Cor 14:37; 2 Cor 7:8; Col 4:16; 1 Thess 5:27; 2 Thess 3:14; 2 Pet 3:16; Rev 1:3). We see Jesus' words quoted as Scripture (1 Tim 5:18b), and Paul warns the Corinthians "not to go beyond what is written" (1 Cor 4:6), meaning God's written word.

The point is—in case you missed it—that Paul's instructions about women not teaching or having authority over men were given in an authoritative apostolic letter, to a church in Ephesus that *had* the written authoritative apostolic word (at least some of it),[14] and yet Timothy and the male elders were still to teach the letter's content (1 Tim 3:2, 4:11, 5:17, 6:2c). And the very thing they were to do was what the women were not to do.

It is hard to see that their situation was very different from ours, except that we have a *collection* of authoritative documents that record the apostolic testimony, which is now more accessible to most people in most parts of the world. This is a difference of degree, not of kind, and certainly not sufficient grounds to reject the plain meaning of this text.

---

13 This includes clear quotations introduced with formulas like "It is written", but also includes echoes, allusions, themes, references to people, places, events, and so on.

14 At least Paul's earlier letter of Ephesians and his first letter to Timothy.

3. Subjective reasons

This brings us to the reasons I most often hear for rejecting the current day application of these verses: either "It's just not fair" or "I feel called to the ministry of preaching".

These statements reflect deeply held personal convictions and emotions and at that level they cannot be argued with. If someone feels something is unfair, they *feel* it is unfair. If a person feels called to preach, they *feel* called to preach. Those feelings are real. But they are not to decide the matter.

If God is a God of perfect justice then his Spirit-inspired word will teach only what is just. We cannot decide independently of Scripture, on the basis of some 'equal opportunity' or 'individual rights' principle, that it would be unjust to allow men to do something that women are not to do, and then use *our* 'justice rule' as a sieve to remove anything in *God's* word that assigns women and men different responsibilities.

Also, whatever we make of subjective 'calls', the objective written word of God must always be our guide no matter how strongly we feel led in our hearts. If there is a conflict, even though we may not like it or even understand it, we must submit to the word of our heavenly Father. It is his will, not ours, that constitutes obedience and we are to pray that he will help us conform to his good and loving will.

A personal conviction, however strong and however well intentioned, should never override the plain sense of Scripture.

What about contexts other than church?

But in hearing and obeying God's word we must take care not to be like Eve in the garden, who took God's command "You shall not eat" (Gen 2:17) and added to it "neither shall you touch" (3:3) just for good measure!

As we have already seen, there are repeated examples in the

New Testament where God used women to teach and encourage his people—young and old, male and female—and where the restrictions of 1 Timothy 2 did not apply. There is a simple reason for this: those situations did not involve the ongoing, authoritative doctrinal instruction of the church gathering, through the exposition and proclamation of Scripture and the apostolic message. Rather, they were private situations, family situations, instances of prophecy, prayer or singing, or the focused instruction of women. And these are just a few examples of how women (and men who are not authorized teachers) can contribute to building up God's household by speaking God's truth in activities that are not the formal ongoing instruction on view in 1 Timothy 2 (cf. 1 Tim 2:7; 4:11, 13, 16; 5:17; 6:2c-3).

Similarly, today we should hope to see women (and men) teaching and encouraging one another in private conversations, within the family, through prophecy, prayer and singing when the community gathers, and in ministries specifically targeting women and children. Women might also encourage the church gathering with accounts of answered prayer, missionary reports, book reviews, ideas for mission, and other matters. It might also be appropriate for women to address para-church conferences on matters in which they have particular expertise, and where the context is no longer the local church community.

I think there is also a place for women to contribute to academic discussion, where ideas are presented and weighed in the (rather impersonal) world of scholarship, and not in the familial local gathering. In a similar vein, women can write books (as I have done). They may be read by men, but it is a context in which you the reader can hear and weigh the author's thoughts and agree or disagree as you see fit, in a private (and admittedly one-way) conversation that lasts as long as the book remains open.

My point is that we must not "go beyond what is written"

(1 Cor 4:6). We must not close more doors than God's word, in its wisdom and goodness, closes.

How to conduct ourselves in God's household

We have covered a lot of territory. We have seen that we are to pray for all people, especially those in high places—for their good and for their salvation. We have seen that Christians are to live quiet and godly lives, which pleases God. We have seen that men are to ensure that male aggression does not hinder their prayers, and that the same unity that characterizes God's mission is expressed in the local church. We have seen that Christian women are to define themselves by quiet living and good deeds, not by flashy physical appearance. And we have worked our way through a handful of verses that have brought more heat and conflict to Christian fellowship in recent years than possibly any others.

As it turns out, we have found that what this passage is saying is not that complicated—although admittedly it *is* rather confronting and countercultural.

This passage limits the participation of women in one area of church life—but it should not leave women out on a limb in terms of ministry opportunities. There is much more that can and needs to be done than stepping into a pulpit—both by men *and* women.

The key to accepting this teaching actually lies at the heart of the chapter itself. It is the character and purpose of the God whose word this is; the Saviour God, who desires the very best for all people—that they might be saved and come to the knowledge of his truth; and whose Son took on human nature—yet was without sin—and gave his life as a ransom for women and men without regard to gender or race or wealth or station in life.

If nothing else, 1 Timothy 2 tells us that God is *for* us, and so we can know that what his word says is good for us—not only for this present life but also for the life to come.

3 | HEAD TO HEAD: 1 CORINTHIANS 11

O N 31 MARCH 2002, THE Queen Mother died peacefully in her sleep at the grand age of 101. She had seen the beginnings of two centuries and all the changes in between. Seven months earlier, on 11 September 2001, almost 3000 people died in coordinated terrorist attacks carried out by extremist Muslims across the USA.

Except for the loss of life, the two events couldn't seem further apart. But strangely, they both brought one particular issue to talkback radio, the front pages of newspapers, and the TV news: whether women should or should not cover their heads.

In the months following September 11, Muslim head coverings became a familiar sight and topic in the media. We grew accustomed to images of Afghani women covered from head to toe in blue *burqas*. We heard disturbing stories of veiled women in Sydney being verbally abused in the street because they were recognizably Muslim. Politicians and school principals began thinking out loud about banning the *hijab*. Young Australian Muslim women, including recent converts, gave interviews and wrote letters to newspapers about why they chose to veil or not to veil.

But it was not just the Islamic practice that made the news. A

'Christian' practice also made global headlines: the question of hats at the Queen Mother's funeral. This posed such a fashion and cultural dilemma that, according to my recollection, an official announcement from the palace was needed. It stated that although women had always worn hats in royal church services in the past, this time they did not have to. Women could choose to hat or not to hat. Some did, some did not.

Chapter 11 of Paul's first letter to the Corinthians also deals with what women wear on their heads. To most of us, the issues he raises seem as foreign to us as hats at royal funerals and the experience of young Muslim women. Culturally, it is a world away.

So what do we make of 1 Corinthians 11 in this day and age? Is there anything in it for us as modern Christian women and men?

At first glance

Let us start by reading the relevant section of 1 Corinthians 11:

> [2]Now I commend you because you remember me in everything and maintain the traditions even as I delivered them to you. [3]But I want you to understand that the head of every man is Christ, the head of a wife is her husband, and the head of Christ is God. [4]Every man who prays or prophesies with his head covered dishonours his head, [5]but every wife who prays or prophesies with her head uncovered dishonours her head, since it is the same as if her head were shaven. [6]For if a wife will not cover her head, then she should cut her hair short. But since it is disgraceful for a wife to cut off her hair or shave her head, let her cover her head. [7]For a man ought not to cover his head, since he is the image and glory of God, but woman is the glory of man. [8]For man was not made from woman, but woman from man. [9]Neither was man created for woman, but woman for man. [10]That is why a wife ought

to have a symbol of authority on her head, because of the angels. [11]Nevertheless, in the Lord woman is not independent of man nor man of woman; [12]for as woman was made from man, so man is now born of woman. And all things are from God. [13]Judge for yourselves: is it proper for a wife to pray to God with her head uncovered? [14]Does not nature itself teach you that if a man wears long hair it is a disgrace for him, [15]but if a woman has long hair, it is her glory? For her hair is given to her for a covering. [16]If anyone is inclined to be contentious, we have no such practice, nor do the churches of God. (1 COR 11:2-16)

This is the second of three New Testament texts that deal with the responsibilities of women and men within the Christian assembly. The remaining text is 1 Corinthians 14, which we will look at in the next chapter as it logically follows on from this section in Paul's letter. All three texts can strike us as particularly confronting, controversial and countercultural given our (often subconscious) feminist sensitivities and agendas.

But although we may have to work hard to understand and apply them, they come to us as God's word, and it is incumbent upon us to hear God's word above all other cultural and personal voices. Of course, our study should be informed by the best that other disciplines have to offer—like linguistics and lexicology, ancient history and archaeology—but even their insights must sit under God's word and not over it. We cannot allow the science of humans to eclipse the word of God.

Since we looked at 1 Timothy 2 in the last chapter, it seems appropriate to begin our study of 1 Corinthians 11:2-16 with a few points of comparison.

The first thing to notice is that this passage is more difficult to understand. It is more than twice the length of 1 Timothy 2:8-15, which means there is more to get our heads around. As it happens, the argument is also more complex.

Another difficulty is that cultural factors in the 1 Corinthians text are more evident. Unlike Muslim head coverings and royal funerals, 1 Corinthians comes from a totally different culture from ours, and is also separated from us by almost 20 centuries. And even modern occurrences of things like prophecy and head coverings are not common in evangelical Christian circles.

But having said that, there are some obvious similarities between this text and 1 Timothy 2.

For starters, Paul wrote them both. Both are delivered as authoritative expressions of his apostolic will, and set in the context of wider church practice. Both are concerned with the conduct of men *and* women. Both are concerned with what women wear, and with their hair. Both refer to childbirth and procreation. There is a concern in both for decency and propriety as opposed to disgrace. Both expect women to be present and participating in the church gathering. Both teach that a person's participation and contribution in church is determined in part by their gender. And both passages refer to Adam and Eve and the creation accounts of Genesis, and the fact that Adam (or the man) was made first and the woman second.

Despite this considerable overlap, there is one significant difference or apparent contradiction: the command for women to be quiet in 1 Timothy 2, and the expectation in 1 Corinthians 11 that women will speak in church as they pray and prophesy. Quiet in one, not quiet in the other.

But, as we saw in the last chapter, there is actually nothing in 1 Timothy 2 to prevent women praying and prophesying in church. Paul only says that women are not to teach or have authority over men. They are to *learn* not teach, and *be submissive* not exercise authority. That is, the prohibition on speaking applies only to certain activities, and limited ones at that. So Paul has not forgotten 1 Corinthians 11 when he writes 1 Timothy 2, and he has not changed his mind. There is no contradiction because the texts are addressing different activities.

A closer look

1 Corinthians 11 contains more that is unfamiliar to us as modern readers than 1 Timothy 2, and with that unfamiliarity comes the temptation to get distracted. What does Paul mean by 'prophecy'? What *did* the head covering look like? What do angels have to with it? How long is long hair and when does it become a disgrace for men? What do these things all mean? In fact, there are so many tantalizing questions and distractions that it is easy to miss the wood for the trees. We can get so caught up in these issues that we miss the main one.

But we are going to put them aside to start with and look at the main issue.

First, we need to put our text in context. In the preceding chapters, Paul has answered questions about sex and marriage and food offered to idols, and he has held up his own and Christ's denial of personal rights and freedom for the sake of others' salvation as the model for Christian conduct. At the beginning of chapter 11, he reminds the Corinthians of the example they are to follow (v. 1).

Paul then congratulates the Corinthians for putting into practice "the traditions" he had previously passed on to them (v. 2), before revisiting some of these in light of issues on the ground in Corinth. The first of these is what differences *are* to exist between men and women when they pray and prophesy in church (vv. 3-16). The second concerns differences that are *not* to exist between the rich and the poor at the communal meal (vv. 17-34).

In the following chapters, Paul answers queries that have arisen about the different gifts and the participation of all believers in the worship gathering (1 Corinthians 12-14). He then revisits the most important tradition under threat, which was the gospel, and the implications of Jesus' resurrection (1 Cor 15:3-5ff).

Now, if we take a bird's-eye view of these chapters (especially 8-14) to see if there are broader themes that might help us understand what Paul is saying about women and men, I think two related themes appear. They are:

1. The potential for what we have been given in Christ—freedom, gifts, etc.—to be used to the detriment of another person.
2. How the differences we find in the Christian community affect the unity of Christ's body, for good and for ill.

Paul's answer to the first is that self-promotion, self-expression, personal rights and freedom are not the measures we are to use in deciding what is right and wrong—rather, the measures are self-denial of rights and loving self-sacrifice. The answer to the second is that God-given differences are to enhance Christian unity rather than destroy it, whereas differences that are human in origin will inevitably divide.

So that is the broader context of 1 Corinthians 11. When we come to the text itself, the key verse is verse 3, which is Paul's starting point. It lays the foundation for what follows. If we can crack this verse, we will be well on the way to understanding the remaining 13.

But that is easier said than done. All sides in this debate agree it is a tricky verse, and in recent times we have seen an avalanche of alternative interpretations. Debate has focused on the translation and meaning of three words in the original Greek: the word usually translated 'head', and whether Paul meant 'man' and 'woman', or 'husband' and 'wife'.

Deciding the translation and meaning of these three words is our first task, and that means doing some hard work. But it will be worth it!

1. The meaning of 'head'

The meaning of the word 'head' is central to the metaphor running through this verse. In recent years, those wanting identical roles for men and women in the family and in Christian ministry have argued that this word 'head' (*kephalē*) means 'source', and not 'authority over' as it has historically been understood.

They argue that just as we might refer to the source of a river being the head of the river, when Paul uses this word here and elsewhere, it means 'source' or 'origin' and does not entail a relationship of authority. Understood like this, the two New Testament passages that use 'head' for the relationship of men to women (here and Ephesians 5:23) become passages about *origins* and not *authority*. This being the case, these passages say nothing more than Genesis 2 says, where woman was made from the man's rib—which, they would say, is also only about origins. It has nothing more to say about authority than the statement "I came from my mother's womb".

From this they conclude that these texts are about *where* we came from, not *how* we are to relate. Having concluded that, it is a short step to say that the different gender responsibilities in these passages simply reflect first-century culture and are not relevant today.

However, three things tell us that 'head' (*kephalē*) does not mean 'source' here.

The first is that in recent years, extensive studies of this Greek word in ancient literature show that it was most often used literally, where it referred to a physical head (i.e. the one on your shoulders) or the top or end of something (e.g. a column). It was also used figuratively, in which case it usually meant 'authority over'. These studies cast doubts about whether this word ever had the meaning of 'source' except in the sense of 'nourishment'—as in 'the head is the source of nourishment for the body (or river)'.

Secondly, it is clear from Paul's use of this word elsewhere that it means 'authority over' or 'leader', and that even when the idea of nourishment is prominent, that of authority is also present (i.e. Eph 4:15; Col 2:19; cf. Eph 1:22, 5:23; Col 1:18, 2:10).

Finally, even if we were to substitute 'source' for 'head' in verse 3, it just does not make theological sense. It would then say, "But I want you to realize that the source of every man is Christ, and the source of the woman is man, and the source of Christ is God".[1] And if we understand 'source' to mean a similar thing in each of the three phrases, we end up with a Christ who was created rather than eternally begotten of the Father, and every man being made from Christ the same way that woman was made from man—that is, taken *out of him* (v. 8).

Hopefully you will recognize that these are wildly unbiblical ideas! God's word tells us that man was made from dust, not from the divine substance (Gen 2:7). And to say that the source of Christ is God in the same way that man is the source of woman is to go down the track of an ancient heresy called Arianism, similar to what Jehovah's Witnesses believe today: that Christ was created rather than eternally pre-existent.

Neither is Paul making a subtle distinction—as some claim he is—about the origins of the *incarnate Christ* as opposed to the *divine Son*. In 1 Corinthians alone, not to mention his other letters, Paul is happy to use the title 'Christ' for the eternal, pre-existent Son who became incarnate and is now raised as Lord, which shows that such a distinction cannot be made (1 Cor 8:6; 10:4, 9; 15:23-28; cf. 1:9; see also Rom 1:4; 2 Cor 1:19; Gal 2:20; Eph 1:3-5, 4:13).

So Paul is not talking about origins in 1 Corinthians 11:3. He's using the word 'head' to talk about order and authority in relationships. And so this verse tells us something about the

---

1   I have used the NIV translation here to show what happens if we change 'head' to 'source'. As my following discussion under point 2 explains, I prefer the NIV translation of verse 3 to that offered by the ESV.

relationships of the Trinity, which provides the context for Paul's instructions for men and women. It tells us there is order within the Godhead, and that the persons of the Trinity (at least the first two) relate in some sort of hierarchical relationship.

This is consistent with what we find in Scripture generally. There we see that whilst the Father is fully God, the Son is fully God, and the Holy Spirit (who is the Spirit of the Father and the Son) is fully God, this does not prevent differentiation and order within the Trinity. The full and eternal divinity and sovereignty of each member of the Trinity does not require that they are identical or interchangeable in terms of roles and authority.

One of the fallacies of much feminist ideology is the belief that for two people to be equal, they must do the same thing. There is an assumption that you cannot have differentiation and hierarchy without also having inferiority and superiority of dignity or worth.

But you can, and this is what we find here and elsewhere in God's word.

All three persons of the Godhead share in the same divine being and nature, yet there is an asymmetry within the divine relationships. There is sameness and equality alongside hierarchy and authority. It is not a case of *either* equality *or* order, but *both* equality and sameness, *and* order and difference.

Paul's statement that "the head of Christ is God" is consistent with other parts of Scripture, which relate not only to Jesus' earthly and eschatological ministry as Saviour and Lord, but also to the eternal relations between the Father and the Son (e.g. 1 Cor 15:28; John 3:16-17, 6:38, 8:42; Gal 4:4; Phil 2:5-11). It does not mean that the Son is any less God because of this. It does not mean that he has an inferior status. It simply means that in his love for us and in his love and obedience to his Father, the Son submits himself to the Father and seeks to bring the Father glory in all he does.

So then, what God's word says here in 1 Corinthians 11 about authority and order in relationships has its basis in God himself, and cannot be conveniently dismissed as strange cultural baggage from the first century.

2. 'Man' and 'woman' or 'husband' and 'wife'

This brings us to the second word puzzle in verse 3. If you have ever studied this passage in a Bible study group, you probably struck this problem pretty early on!

Let me explain. Most translations render the first phrase as something like "I want you to understand that the head of every man is Christ". So far, so good. But then it gets tricky because different translations have different things for the second phrase.

Some popular Bible versions say, "and the head of the *woman* is *man*" (or similar).[2] But others say, "the head of a *wife* is *her husband*".[3] Confusing isn't it? How are we meant to work it out if the Bible translators cannot even agree?

The problem for the translators, as we saw with 1 Timothy 2, is that biblical Greek uses the same word for 'man' and 'husband' and the same word for 'woman' and 'wife'. And the problem for us is that it makes a difference to the meaning of the passage. How do we know if it is talking about married couples or men and women generally?

Now if a teenager says to us "I have a really *cool* jumper", the context of the sentence lets us know that she does not mean she has a woollen jumper that keeps her really cool in hot weather. She means that she thinks her woollen jumper is pretty "awesome".

We cope with the fact that the word 'cool' has different meanings in English by using the context to help us work out which meaning is intended.

In the same way, two things in the context here let us know that

---

2   e.g. NIV, NASB, NKJV
3   e.g. ESV; similarly, the NRSV has "the husband is the head of his wife".

Paul is talking about men and women generally, not just husbands and wives.

In the first place, it would be strange for Paul to use the same word to mean 'man' in the first phrase of verse 3, then without explanation switch the meaning to 'husband' in the second phrase. In the absence of any indications to do otherwise, we should translate the same word the same way throughout this tightly knit verse, especially since the repetition of words and ideas seems key to its meaning.

Following on from this, even though headship language is used in Ephesians for the marriage relationship, there is no indication in 1 Corinthians 11:3 that marriage is on view. In fact, translations that use 'husband' and 'wife' have to introduce possessive pronouns (i.e. 'his' or 'her'), which are not in the original, so that their translations read more naturally. It may be that married women in particular come into view later in the passage, but in this summary statement of principle in verse 3, Paul is talking about men and women generally.

The second thing that helps us work out what Paul means by these words in verse 3 is that his statements about human beginnings (vv. 7-9) and future generations (vv. 11-12) relate to men and women generally, making it more likely that his opening statement of principle refers to all men and women, not just the married ones.

We have now done the heavy lifting in regards to the three disputed words of verse 3. We have found it means that the head of the woman is the man. But what does this mean for us today?

Before we think about that, it is important for us to notice what verse 3 does *not* say.

It does not say that *all* women are to submit to *all* men. It is coming at the relationship from the other end. It is about headship rather than submission.

It does not say that women are second-class citizens with less dignity, intelligence, worth or purpose than men. Just as Jesus Christ is not diminished in divinity and glory because he has a head (i.e. God), neither is a woman diminished because she has a head (i.e. man).

At the same time, however, it does not say there is no difference between men and women. The implication is that there is an order in the relationship between men and women that is in some way analogous to that within the Trinity.

And finally, verse 3 doesn't give us any details of what it means that the head of the woman is the man. Rather, it is a summary statement of principle, functioning a bit like a heading (pardon the pun) that informs the rest of the passage. And so it leaves the question of the details hanging.

Does it mean that men should open doors for women? Does it mean that men should pay on dates? Does it mean that women and children get the first seats in lifeboats if the boat is sinking? Does it mean that only men can be CEOs or join the armed forces or lead a nation?

The truth is that this text does not answer these or similar questions one way or the other—nor does the Bible as a whole!

What the New Testament does say on this matter is quite limited. If man is the head of woman, God's word gives us only a handful of examples of how this actually works out in practice.

In this particular passage, it has implications for the different things Christian women and men are to do with their heads when they pray and prophesy in the community gathering.

Looking beyond this passage, the same principle means that in the Christian gathering women are not to teach or have authority over men generally—not just their husbands (1 Timothy 2). The same order of relationship means that women are not to publicly evaluate prophecies (1 Corinthians 14). So in the New Testament there are three explicit implications of male headship for the participation and contribution of women and men in church.

God also teaches that the principle of male headship has implications for the marriage relationship, for both the husband and the wife. Wives are willingly to submit to their husband's leadership, and husbands are lovingly and sacrificially to lead their wives (Ephesians 5; Colossians 3; 1 Peter 3).

Are there further implications beyond these specific examples in the church and in marriage? Well, the Bible does not say, and we can only work with what it does say. Fortunately, we know that God has given us all that is *necessary* for us to live godly lives (2 Pet 1:3).

The best way of thinking about 1 Corinthians 11:3 is to view it as a summary statement. The male headship Paul is talking about in this statement of principle is expressed in specific situations and relationships—namely, in the leadership of the church community and in marriage. If we want to apply the principle beyond that, we must leave the firm ground of Scripture.

It makes sense to me that there would be implications beyond these two scenarios for the way men and women generally relate and help each other become the people God designed us to be. But the New Testament does not explicitly spell these out for us.

One implication might be that the roles and responsibilities a person has within particular relationships might inform the way we relate to them, even though we ourselves are not in those relationships with that person. For example, a female boss might relate to a married male employee in a way that acknowledges the responsibility and authority he exercises in his home, even though as an employee he answers to her. In this regard, I am reminded of the centurion who recognized in Jesus a person like himself—one in authority and under authority—and so treated Jesus accordingly (Matt 8:9). But I am just thinking out loud at this point.

We have spent a lot of time on a single verse, working out the meaning of three key words. This has been hard but essential work, because it provides the framework for Paul's instructions about what men and women are to wear on their heads as they pray and prophesy.

But we are not quite finished with questions of definition yet. There are still two more to answer before we can look at Paul's instructions: what did Paul mean by 'prophesying', and what were the head coverings?

3. The meaning of 'prophesying' then and now

For modern Christians, the debate about the nature of prophecy is almost as hot and divisive as the debate about the word 'head'. And our modern debate is complicated by the fact that the New Testament does not give us a definition or 'how-to' guide for prophecy, and that we see a variety of prophetic traditions in the Old Testament, and that even in the first-century world there were different ideas about prophecy.

The best approach then is to describe (rather than define) prophecy in broad terms. So here is an eight-point beginner's guide.

(i) We should not assume that New Testament prophecy is identical to prophecy in the Old Testament. There are at least two differences worth noting.

The first is that there is a difference in authority between much Old Testament and New Testament prophecy, both in regards to the words spoken and the person who spoke them. In the Old Testament, disobedience to the word of a true prophet was equal to disobeying God and came with correspondingly serious consequences (Deut 18:17-19; 1 Kgs 20:35-36). In the New Testament, that is not always the case (Acts 21:4-5,15). Furthermore, in the Old Testament, false prophets were to be put to death; but in the New Testament, prophecies are to be evaluated and even if a prophecy is rejected, the prophet lives to see another day (Deut 18:20; 1 Cor 14:29; 1 Thess 5:19-21; 1 John 4:1-6)!

If you put this diminished authority of New Testament prophecies spoken by regular Christians together with the need for these prophecies to be evaluated, I think it helps to explain why it is okay for women to prophesy but not to evaluate prophecies or to teach and have authority over men. But we will return to this when we look at 1 Corinthians 14.

The second difference lies in the content of prophecy. Broadly speaking, prophecy falls into two categories: *fore*telling future events, and '*forth*-telling' the deeds of God. Much Old Testament prophecy was foretelling future events.[4] This type of prophecy is proved true when it happens (Deut 18:21-22; Jer 28:9). In the New Testament, while there is some prophetic foretelling, the prophecies that are part of Christian meetings do not need the test of time. They can be evaluated then and there (1 Cor 14:29). I take it this is because they are 'forth-telling', or declaring existing truth, rather than predicting what God will do.

(ii) The prophecy on view in 1 Corinthians 11 happens in the Christian gathering and is verbal, audible, and intelligible.

(iii) Genuine prophecy contributes to the growth of the Christian community, either quantitatively by leading to the conversion of visitors, or qualitatively by edifying, encouraging and consoling believers (1 Cor 14:3-5, 24-26, 31). In the first instance this includes revealing the secrets of people's hearts. In the second, it involves the application of divine truth. For both, the proof of authenticity is conformity to the truth of the inspired word of God and to the gospel (1 Cor 12:3; 1 John 4:2-3, 6).

---

4   While foretelling was an obvious element of Old Testament prophecy, if we look closer we find that there is much Old Testament prophecy that is of the 'forth-telling' variety.

(iv) As we saw in my previous chapter, prophecy is different from teaching and preaching, even though there are some similarities in purpose, content and outcome.

(v) Both men and women can prophesy in the church gathering. This is unlike teaching, which is not the responsibility of women or of men who are not gifted to teach (1 Tim 2:12, 3:2).

(vi) The act of prophesying is under the control of the speaker (1 Cor 14:32). It is not involuntary or ecstatic.

(vii) The content of prophecy (if it is genuine) is God-given, and so it can come to a person spontaneously as they sit in church (1 Cor 14:30). But there is no reason why it might not be received earlier and later shared.

(viii) Even if a prophecy is from God, it *need not* be shared (1 Cor 14:30). It is more important to Paul that everything is done in such a way that everyone learns and is encouraged, than for every revelation to be shared. Somewhat surprisingly, he is not concerned if a prophecy never sees the light of day!

The question I hear you asking is, "Does prophecy happen today?" I think it does—or at least it should!

Some years ago at our church, a female missionary shared in the Sunday service what was happening with her work as a missionary doctor in a government-run orphanage in Eastern Europe. She spoke for about ten minutes, and was introduced by the male senior pastor, who also thanked her and prayed for her work at the end.

When she finished I leant over and said to Rob, "That was the closest thing to prophecy I've heard in this church". It was intelligible and verbal. It was public. It was focused on the gospel and what God was doing in her life and through her. It was absolutely inspiring. We all learnt things about God's faithfulness, and about suffering for the sake of the gospel. It carried these truths deep into our hearts. Many of us were rebuked for our comfortable cost-less Christianity, and encouraged as she reflected on certain Scriptures that had given her comfort and strength.

But it was clearly not the sermon. The sermon (which was delivered from the pulpit, not the central microphone) followed this 'missionary update', and was given by a male leader of the congregation.

Now I do not know if Paul or the Corinthians would have called this prophecy, but it fits with the broad description I have just given, and I think if we saw more of this sort of thing in our churches then we would all benefit.

It is easy for us to get stuck on the countercultural gender issues of 1 Corinthians 11 and unwittingly miss something else that might be equally countercultural in our evangelical churches—which is that women and men who are not gifted teachers can be gifted in other ways and used by God to build his people. And we are the poorer if we prevent that from happening.

4. The meaning of the head coverings

And that brings us to the fashion part of this passage. What is Paul talking about when he says men are to have their heads uncovered and women their heads covered?

We could fill another room with the books written on this topic and be no clearer in our minds when we had finished reading than when we began.

Once again, it is important to work out what the real issue is here. As it turns out, the real issue is not so much the identity of the actual head covering as what it means, and why Paul wants women to wear it and men not to wear it. It is the meaning of wearing or not wearing it rather than the head covering itself that is most important.

But to work out the meaning we must first identify the head covering. There are three possibilities: a garment (a veil, shawl or cloak); an attitude of mind; or a hairstyle. You will find older books expending a great amount of ink defending one or other of these.

But in recent years there has been a breakthrough in ancient history research that suggests the head covering in question was most likely a veil worn by married women.[5] This veil symbolized the husband's authority within marriage. From 1 Corinthians 11 we can see that it also functioned as an appropriate and meaningful symbol for Christians of the authority and order of gender relationships.

It was a piece of clothing but it was a piece of clothing *with meaning*. And that is not such a difficult concept to grasp.

When I was doing my nursing training many years ago, nurses all wore something on their heads. All student nurses wore white starched caps. First-year nurses had one red stripe centre-front, second-years had two, and third-years had three stripes and lace trim around the edge. When you graduated and became a sister, you got to wear these flying-nun-type veils, which were a nuisance because they got caught on curtains and sheets, but which showed you were at the top of the ladder.

What nurses wore on their heads said something about their authority and who they were in relation to others in terms of their authority. And it was like that in Corinth. The veil in question was a piece of clothing with a well-recognized meaning—and that meaning had something to do with authority.

And why does Paul want married women to wear this piece of clothing and men not to wear it?

Six reasons for Paul's instructions[6]

1. Godhead (vv. 4-6)

The most fundamental reason is that this veil symbolically represented the ordered relationships between men and women

---

5   For example, see Bruce Winter, *Roman Wives, Roman Widows*, Eerdmans, Grand Rapids, 2003, pp. 77-96.

6   These six reasons are similar to those identified by Mary Kassian in her book *Women, Creation and the Fall*, Crossway, Westchester, 1990, pp. 97-100.

that reflect the relationships of the Trinity. Paul wanted husbands and wives to look different, because by doing so they reflected the ordered relationships that God created them for, which, in turn, reflect the relationships of the Godhead.

When a man covered his head while praying and prophesying—possibly motivated by misguided spiritual one-upmanship—he was in effect denying his responsibilities as a man by dressing like a woman. When he did so he dishonoured his head (v. 4), both his physical head and his metaphorical relational head, Christ.

When a married woman did not cover her head—perhaps because she was mistakenly taking her newfound freedom in Christ too far—she brought shame on her literal head and on her metaphorical relational head, her husband, because she was in effect denying her relational responsibilities as a wife (v. 5). She might as well have turned up dressed like an adulteress or prostitute (v. 6)!

So Paul wants men and women to dress and behave in a way that is consistent with the roles and responsibilities they have within marriage, and to be content with the ordered pattern of relationships that God has ordained, which reflects the relations of the Godhead.

2. Creation (vv. 7-9)

The next reason Paul gives for his instructions presents a minefield of political incorrectness for our feminist sensitivities. It is based on the differences in the order and manner in which God created the sexes, as well as differences in the reasons he created them.

Paul kicks off this argument by saying the reason a man ought not to cover his head is that "he is the image and glory of God, but woman is the glory of man"—and implicitly, this is also why she should cover her head (v. 7).

Is Paul suggesting that woman is not made in the image of God?

You will be relieved to know this is *not* what he means! If that had been his meaning he would have said, "he is the image and glory of God, but woman is the *image and* glory of man".

But he does not say that.

Paul leaves out the 'image' statement in the second phrase. In repeating the statement about glory but not the one about image, Paul creates a clunkiness that makes it clear his point is about 'glory', not about in whose image woman was made. This is hardly surprising. As a former Pharisee and Jewish Bible scholar, Paul knew that both men and women were created in God's image!

But that may still leave us with our feminist hackles up, and wondering why he says woman is the glory of man. Fortunately, he does not leave us guessing.

Woman is the glory of man because she was taken out of him and because she was made for him (vv. 8-9). In both her origins and her purpose, the woman corresponds to the man.

She was made from bone of his bone and flesh of his flesh, and she was made for him—not he for her. This does not mean that women were made as playthings or domestic slaves for men or as incubators and carers for his children.

It means that he was created first—he was the firstborn with all the responsibilities that being the firstborn entailed—and that she was made to help him in those responsibilities.

Of course, Paul is drawing on Genesis 1 and 2 and the beginnings of the relationship between the sexes, before human sin and divine judgement introduced pain and frustration into that relationship.

By looking backwards to human beginnings, Paul tells us that an ordered pattern of relationship between the sexes is part of the way God made us. As I noted in my previous chapter, it is not a result of the Fall, nor is it a first-century cultural oddity that does not concern us now.

Indeed, neither of these two main reasons behind Paul's instructions—the pattern of relationships within the Trinity nor the principles and implications of Genesis 1 and 2—can be restricted to any particular time or culture. They are universally true. They do not have a shelf life. They are 'transcultural'—true for all time.

Paul is saying that when it comes to the relationships of men and women, the order of relationships in creation and within the Godhead counts—no matter what culture you find yourself in. And he spells out for the people of Corinth that this order means men and women are to behave differently when they gather as the family of God, and they are to display those differences clearly.

When they do that, man brings glory to his head and a wife brings glory to hers.

But just in case the men in Corinth (and today) read verses 7-9 and get a rush of blood to the head, Paul brings them back down to earth with an equally important reality (vv. 11-12).

There is no sense that men are better than women, because neither is independent of the other. Not only are they *both* made in the image of God (v. 7) but they both *need* each other. Woman may come from man but man is born of woman. Woman may have been created as a helper suitable for man, but without her man cannot fill the earth or subdue it. Man and woman need each other. They have a common origin (i.e. God), and each is a gift from God to the other (v. 12).

And besides, as the summary statement of verse 3 makes clear from the outset, *every* man is under the headship of Christ.

3. "Because of the angels" (v. 10)

The third reason Paul gives for his instructions comes in a notoriously difficult verse that we skipped over a moment ago (v. 10). As convenient as it would be simply to note how difficult it is and then move on, we need to try to understand Paul's point. This is how I see it.

- Although the word 'sign' or 'symbol' is not in the original Greek text, the head covering Paul has been discussing did function as a sign or symbol of authority on the wife's head. So I take it that the verse is talking about the head covering.

- The authority the veil represented was that of the husband, as Paul's previous explanation makes clear (vv. 5-9).
- The reference to angels is a new idea, and another reason for the wife to have authority on her head.
- Because it is a new idea, after which Paul discusses reciprocal elements in the relationship of woman and man (vv. 11-12), it is possible that this verse acts as a bridge that holds together the order *and* mutual dependence of women and men.
- Angels have already been mentioned twice in 1 Corinthians: they are witnesses of what happens on earth (1 Cor 4:9; cf. 1 Tim 5:21; 1 Pet 1:12), and they will be judged by Christians on the last day (1 Cor 6:3).
- The conclusion I draw from all this is that by accepting and demonstrating her place within God's order of gender relationships, a wife also demonstrates her place in the greater order of creation as someone made in the image of God who one day, along with men, will judge angels (cf. Heb 2:5-8).
- Thus, while the head covering functions as a sign of her husband's authority, and must be worn when a wife prays and prophesies in public, her willing acceptance of his authority affirms her equal dignity and valued (but different) role in this creation, and her participation in the next.

That is my explanation of this difficult verse. There are other explanations that are similar, and some that are very different. The truth is that certainty on this enigmatic verse might elude us until the day we come to judge the angels! Whatever the case, it makes little difference to Paul's main point about the different conduct of women and men when they pray and prophesy.

4. Nature (vv. 14-15)

Paul gives three further reasons for his instructions. The first is that "nature itself" teaches that men and women ought to do different things with their hair (v. 14). Is Paul simply saying, "This is the way things are done around here, so don't rock the cultural boat", or is he saying something more significant?

Elsewhere when Paul uses this word 'nature', he is not talking about social customs but about an innate God-given sense of what God requires (Rom 1:26, 2:14).

His point seems to be that people intuitively know men and women are different and should therefore look different, and that those differences have their foundation in the created order. A similar thing might be the way we intuitively know that adults should look out for children. This correspondence between what is right and our intuition is to be expected. It makes sense that, in God's providential internal wiring of us, our sense of how things ought to be would correspond with his intentions for us.

5. Tradition (v. 2)

The fifth reason Paul gives for his instructions is found right back at the beginning of the passage where he praises the Corinthians for sticking to "the traditions" he taught them during his earlier visit (v. 2).

We have to understand that when Paul talks about traditions, he does not mean what we mean when we talk about traditions. He is not talking about a New Testament equivalent of Easter eggs and Mother's Day—practices that have been around for a long time and are nice ideas, but have no deeper meaning.

In the New Testament, the word 'traditions' is almost technical jargon for the body of teaching that was/is the Christian faith (2 Thess 2:15, 3:6; cf. 1 Cor 11:23, 15:3). It was these traditions that the apostles passed on to churches and which defined true Christianity. They were commands to be obeyed, not window-dressing.

6. Universal practice (v. 16)

Paul's final reason finishes off this section of his letter. He insists that what he is saying is not up for debate because it is common practice in all the churches, and there is no other way of doing things (v. 16).[7]

Paul is not asking the Corinthians to do something that no-one else was doing. He is insisting they remain in fellowship with all the other churches of God by doing what they all did in maintaining the God-given responsibilities and distinctions between the sexes.

Paul leaves no room for the appeals for toleration and diversity that we hear in our modern churches in debates about these matters (and sexuality). Paul firmly closes the door on the 'we should be free to do our own thing' approach to this matter. The Corinthians were not free to do their own thing or go their own way. Its theological importance meant there could be no 'freedom' on this matter—as there might be, for example, on eating meat offered to idols.

So with these strong words, Paul brings his discussion to a close.

Uncovering cultural meanings

So how does this passage apply today? If men and women have been created with differences and with a relational order that is to be expressed visually when we gather together to pray and prophesy, does this mean that women should be wearing head coverings today?

I have only once been to a church that did anything like what Paul is talking about here.

As a twenty-something-year-old backpacker, I visited a church that met in a school in Worthing in the south of England. As I got to the door I realized that all the women were wearing head-

---

7   I find the ESV translation of this verse to be slightly confusing. The gist of it is: "If anyone wants to be contentious by doing 'x', we have no such practice as 'x', nor do the churches of God"—where 'x' is some practice other than what Paul has outlined. The NIV is clearer: "If anyone wants to be contentious about this, we have no other practice—nor do the churches of God."

scarves. Since I did not have one with me I started walking away, because I did not want to offend anyone. But a few people ran after me and asked me to come back in and join them. It was more important to them that they welcomed an outsider than that I had my head covered. God bless them! It was one of the most memorable and thought-provoking church services I have ever been to (and we will return to it in the next chapter in the context of weighing prophecies).

Were these women right in veiling their heads? Is that what this text requires?

Well, clearly there are people who believe it does. And if your understanding of 1 Corinthians 11 and your conscience lead you to that conclusion, then you should cover your head. You are certainly not *dis*obeying the word of God if you do, and you will not be sinning against your conscience just for the sake of fitting in (which you may be doing if you don't cover your head).

The reason I do not come to that conclusion myself is that it is difficult to apply the text *exactly*, because veils do not have the meaning today that they had in the first century.

In actual fact, veils today more often mean the exact opposite from what Paul intends. Friends familiar with Muslim culture, which is primarily where veils are worn these days, tell me their head coverings are a sign of *subservience* and *in*equality rather than a visual reminder of *authority* that occurs within a relationship of *equal* worth and dignity.

But if we steer clear of veils because of their meaning within Islam and opt instead for hats, we strike a similar problem.

This is because hats no longer communicate an acceptance of God's order of gender relationships (if they ever did). These days, women wear hats because they are sun-smart or dressed up to go to the horse races or to a royal wedding or funeral. A hat is a sign that a woman is sensible or fashionable! So hats will not do either.

The fact is there is no piece of clothing that functions as a cultural equivalent to the first-century Graeco-Roman head covering. Brides today might wear veils on their wedding day, but that is because they make a pretty picture and not because of what they symbolize. Besides, the veil is usually history as soon as the photos are taken, and if not then, certainly by the time the happy couple leave the reception!

In Western cultures, there is no *garment* that says, "I'm a married woman and I'm *happy* to be a married woman and to accept the order and authority that God's pattern of relationships gives to my husband".

But this does not mean there are *no* cultural symbols that say those things! We need to be students of our culture. And although our culture is eclectic, there are a few practices that touch on this matter.

For example, the wedding ring is still a sign of being married, although perhaps the power of that sign is more apparent in the breach than in the observance—just think of the person who has deliberately stopped wearing a wedding ring, or the deserted spouse whose right to wear a ring has been removed.

Admittedly, in our egalitarian feminist culture the *different* responsibilities of a husband and wife are not readily symbolized by the rings that each wears. And since many couples now use reciprocally identical marriage vows, we might wonder whether wedding bands convey male headship at all. But understood correctly, they might do so.

I also happen to think that the convention of women taking their husband's last name when they marry is still a culturally meaningful way of showing that a wife is joining her husband in a newly constituted family of which he is the head. Certainly, those feminists who refuse to take their husband's name show that this is exactly what the convention means.

So when women do not take their husband's name, or when a couple combines their names to create a double-barrelled family name, there is a tacit rejection of at least some aspects of a husband's leadership. Of course, a name change is not a visual symbol in the way that veils were in Paul's day, but it is nonetheless a culturally recognized symbol of a husband's headship.

This might change as culture changes but for the time being, Christian women and men need to think carefully about whether their decisions about last/family names best express their joyful acceptance of God's pattern for their marriage relationship.

However, if we think the significance of this text for us hangs on the existence of a similar cultural *symbol*, we have missed the point. Paul's concern was not really about the abuse of *symbols* by men and women. The problem was what their conduct said about their identity and their relationships. And so we need to think about how our conduct—as women or men—might bring honour or shame upon ourselves and our relational heads, by affirming or undermining the roles and responsibilities that we have at home and in creation.

For example, this might mean some men need to step up to the plate at church and stop being passive observers who shirk their responsibilities. It might also mean that some women/wives need to resist the temptation to take hold of the reins, and instead allow and trust the men to lead *like men*! It is no good for women to lament the absence of male leadership when in fact women have filled the (alleged) vacuum, forcing men to 'depose' them in order to lead. It is also no good for men to lament that they are treated like mute passengers when in fact they will not speak or act!

Participate and differentiate

Let me take us right back almost to where we started when we put our text in context. The problem in Corinth seems to have been that the freedoms these new Christians were enjoying were being expressed to the detriment of others. The men were covering their heads and the wives were uncovering their heads. The irony was that as they did what the other sex was meant to do, they brought shame upon themselves and their relational heads instead of the glory and one-upmanship they were hoping for!

Paul's solution is not to remove all distinctions between men and women but to reiterate those God-given distinctions that are to continue within the body of Christ. These distinctions are *good*. In this case, the distinction concerns the authority and equality that shape Christian marriage and are to be expressed when we meet together as God's family. This order has its origin in God's design for human relationships, and reflects the equal yet asymmetrical relations within the Godhead.

Paul's letter to the Corinthians tells us that some differences and distinctions within Christian fellowship actually destroy what God is building, whereas others support and strengthen it.

We are to strive for the latter kind in our obedience to Christ.

And so perhaps the fuller application to our churches of Paul's message is that we need to work harder to express the God-given differences and distinctions in our fellowship—of gender and of gifts—and work harder to remove the differences and divisions that are not God-given and which arise from our selfish, proud, ambitious hearts, destroying the unity we have as the body of Christ.

4 | THE RIGHT TO REMAIN SILENT: 1 CORINTHIANS 14

SOME YEARS AGO, PERIOD REALITY TV shows were all the rage. People were taken out of their modern environment and placed in situations from a bygone era. One of these shows put people into a 19th-century manor house in England. There was an actual family—mum, dad and the kids—who became the ruling aristocracy and lived 'above stairs', while others became the valets, cooks, gardeners, and servants who lived 'below stairs'.

Part of the drama was that they had to observe the cultural mores of the 19th century. For example, the ruling class had to sit at the dining table and be waited on and ignore the servants who, for their part, had to stand back from the table and could only speak when they were spoken to.

It was interesting that although they took a little time to get used to being waited on, and at first felt quite uncomfortable about ordering people around, the aristocrats very quickly got used to the privileges of wealth and power!

'Below stairs', however, it was a different story. The people who had been assigned as servants really struggled with the whole concept of a two-tiered society. They had to accept whatever demands were made of them, and were almost without the right to their own life, and were certainly without the right to speak their own mind. In fact, talking back cost them their job.

They were modern people raised with modern freedoms, and for many of them the cost of living in another culture that took away those freedoms was simply too much to bear—to the extent that they quit the show rather than accept the cultural demands.

Modern society had ruined them for Victorian culture.

Now many people would say this provides a pretty good parallel to what we find in 1 Corinthians 14; that the distinctions there between men and women were fine in the first century, but do not belong and cannot—indeed, should not—be tolerated in the 21st, not least because they are contrary to the shape of the gospel. They are social customs that have passed their use-by date, and hold nothing more for us than historical curiosity.

But as we have seen already in this book, what can strike us as culturally foreign is not necessarily irrelevant. In the texts we've examined so far, we have seen that the reasons the New Testament gives for the instructions about the conduct and participation of women and men in church are not principally cultural. They do not concern things that are true for just one culture. They are 'transcultural', as they concern the very beginnings of humanity, both before and in the Fall, as well as the eternal relations within the Godhead.

Obvious questions

1 Corinthians 14:26-40 is the third and final New Testament text that deals explicitly with gender relations within the church family. It forms the conclusion of Paul's discussion of the relative merits of prophecy over un-interpreted tongues (1 Corinthians 14), and of his broader discussion of the unity and diversity of the body of Christ, and the sovereign prerogative of God and priority of love in the exercise of gifts (1 Corinthians 12-14).

Here is what Paul writes:

> ²⁶What then, brothers [and sisters]?[1] When you come together, each one has a hymn, a lesson, a revelation, a tongue, or an interpretation. Let all things be done for building up. ²⁷If any speak in a tongue, let there be only two or at most three, and each in turn, and let someone interpret. ²⁸But if there is no-one to interpret, let each of them keep silent in church and speak to himself and to God. ²⁹Let two or three prophets speak, and let the others weigh what is said. ³⁰If a revelation is made to another sitting there, let the first be silent. ³¹For you can all prophesy one by one, so that all may learn and all be encouraged, ³²and the spirits of prophets are subject to prophets. ³³For God is not a God of confusion but of peace.
>
> As in all the churches of the saints, ³⁴the women should keep silent in the churches. For they are not permitted to speak, but should be in submission, as the Law also says. ³⁵If there is anything they desire to learn, let them ask their husbands at home. For it is shameful for a woman to speak in church.
>
> ³⁶Or was it from you that the word of God came? Or are you the only ones it has reached? ³⁷If anyone thinks that he is a prophet, or spiritual, he should acknowledge that the things I am writing to you are a command of the Lord. ³⁸If anyone does not recognize this, he is not recognized. ³⁹So, my brothers [and sisters], earnestly desire to prophesy, and do not forbid speaking in tongues. ⁴⁰But all things should be done decently and in order.
>
> (1 COR 14:26-40)

---

1   The ESV notes elsewhere: "Or *brothers and sisters*. The plural Greek word *adelphoi* (translated 'brothers') refers to siblings in a family. In New Testament usage, depending on the context, *adelphoi* may refer either to men or to both men and women who are siblings (brothers and sisters) in God's family, the church." So also in verse 39.

As we have done in previous chapters, we will begin by asking simple comprehension questions about the verses dealing with women and men (vv. 33b-35). This way we can let the text speak on its own before we come to it with the many other valid questions it raises. There are four obvious questions:

(i) What are women not to do?
(ii) What are women to do?
(iii) When and where are women to do these things?
(iv) Why are women to do these things?

Reading the answers straight off the page, they are:

(i) Women are not permitted to speak.
(ii) Women are to keep silent and be in submission, and if there is anything they want to learn they are to ask their husbands at home.
(iii) Women are to be silent in all the churches of the saints.
(iv) Women are to do this because of the Law, and because it is shameful for a woman to speak in church.

Obvious difficulties

Wow! I don't know about you but as a new Christian, the first time I heard this passage I couldn't believe my ears. And to be honest, I'm not sure it was only the *first* time!

I think my reaction represents the first major difficulty we hit when we come to this passage: for most if not all of us, we have a severe cultural knee jerk. Now, there are occasions when our knee-jerk reactions to God's word can offer us spiritual comfort. I have in mind those times when we are shocked by the counter-cultural demands of obedience or kingdom values, but can see that the excuses and resistance in our hearts are just our sinful selves stalling for time. So while we might react to challenges to our materialism or to our speeding on the roads ("It's not *really* wrong; everyone's doing it!"), or to the way we treat our parents, our inner struggle is encouraging proof of the Spirit's work and a dawning acknowledgement that we know we need to change.

But somehow when the Bible starts dealing with men and women, we fall off the horse. Most of us, particularly women, have been taught to be super sensitive about gender injustice and equal opportunity. This sort of passage pushes all our buttons and sounds all our alarms, and our knee-jerk response is, "You've got to be joking!"

That's our most obvious difficulty—a response in us.

The next difficulty is a problem with the text. It seems flatly to contradict 1 Corinthians 11, which we just looked at. How can women be permitted to pray and prophesy in one chapter and then three chapters later not be permitted to speak at all? The passages can't both be right. Either women can pray and prophesy or they must be silent. They can't do both.

Another obvious difficulty is working out which "Law" Paul is talking about. If he has some ancient Rabbinic or Roman law in mind then these verses are nothing more than an interesting history lesson. They are like my mother's decades-old little crimson book of etiquette: quaint, eye-opening and often funny, but obsolete.

Alternatively, if Paul means an Old Testament law or just the Old Testament generally, where does it say that women aren't to speak in church? (In fact, did they even have 'church' in the Old Testament?) That is our third difficulty.

The fourth is working out which women Paul has in mind. All women? Just married women? A few women who are making too much noise in the Corinthian church? Which women does Paul mean? This question is complicated, as it was in the two earlier texts, by the fact that the Greek uses the same word for 'woman' and for 'wife' (*gunē*). Paul may be speaking about married women only—in which case all unmarried women can breathe a sigh of relief—or he may have all women in mind. The only way of telling if the word means 'woman' or 'wife' is from the context, and that might not give us the precision we are looking for. So does this refer to all women, all wives, or perhaps just all extroverts?

Possible easy solutions

Given these obvious difficulties, how are we to approach 1 Corinthians 14:33b-35?

1. Remove the passage

If you read some commentaries on 1 Corinthians, you will find complicated theories about how verses 34-35 weren't in Paul's original letter but were added by someone else some time later.

The theory goes something like this: a scribe copying a manuscript of Paul's original letter made a note in the margin of the text (the way we might in our own Bibles), which was then mistakenly copied into the text itself by the next generation of scribes. The technical name for the added bit of text is 'interpolation'.

If this is the case, we are obliged to remove the offending verses in the knowledge that Paul never wrote them and so they are not God's authoritative word to us. We can forget the whole thing.

This theory has the advantage of being clean and simple. Its disadvantage is that the evidence does not support it! All the manuscripts on which our New Testaments are based have these verses—even the earliest ones—so there is no good reason to see them as a later addition. While a few manuscripts have the two verses in a slightly different position (i.e. following verse 40), there is *no* existing manuscript from which they are missing altogether. The 'interpolation' theory lacks any evidence that these verses were not always part of Paul's letter. In fact, all the evidence points in the other direction.

All the more so because, as we will see from the structure, vocabulary and subject matter, these verses blend in with what goes before and what comes after in chapter 14. They don't look like a different patch of fabric that has just been stuck on and does not fit.

And of course there are strong similarities between verses 34-35 and 1 Timothy 2:11-12, which is to be expected if Paul wrote them both.

So although it might be a neat solution to say that Paul never wrote these words, it is not an escape route open to us.

2. Relativise the passage

Another easy way of getting around the difficulties of this passage is to put it down to first-century Graeco-Roman culture, or a particular problem in the Corinthian church, and say that if Paul were around today he would say something very different to us.

For example, we might say that the prohibition against women speaking was like the prohibition against servants speaking when they served dinner in Victorian England. Although it was accepted practice in its original cultural setting, it is so no longer—in fact, it is now contrary to our culture—and thus no longer applies.

More than that (to continue this line of argument), the prohibition denies the shape of the gospel that we find in Galatians 3:28: "There is neither Jew nor Greek, there is neither slave nor free, there is no male and female, for you are all one in Christ Jesus". This verse, some claim, says that any distinctions on the basis of gender are removed once we become Christians. Except for their obvious physical differences, men and women are the same and are to do the same things. Gender role differences belong to the distortion of male and female relationships that occurred in the Fall, and they are now reversed in Christ.

In fairness, at first glance we might think this is indeed what Galatians 3:28 is saying—particularly if it is quoted apart from its immediate context, as it often is in arguments where it is used to deny any differences between men and women in marriage and in ministry.

But if we look again at Galatians 3:28, there are two problems with this understanding.

The first is that, in context, this verse is not addressing women's ministry or the roles and responsibilities of men and women (as I mentioned in chapter 2). It is addressing our common relationship to Christ. Whereas under the Old Covenant and in Roman society there were religiously and socially accepted categories that kept people apart, in Christ all people are united. We all share the same experience of salvation.

This is a wonderful truth! There is no inner or outer circle in the household of faith. There are no tiers. No dress circle and stalls. No privileged customers. No VIPs. In Christ we are all equally sons of God[2] through faith, all baptized into Christ, all one in Christ, and all Abraham's offspring and heirs according to promise (Gal 3:25-29). It is our unity and common experience of grace that is occupying Paul's mind. He is not addressing the roles and relationship of men and women in the family and church.

This leads us to the second problem with this understanding of Galatians 3:28: in those places where Paul *does* deal with relationships of men and women, he *does* make distinctions on the basis of gender. In other words, Paul would have to disagree with himself if Galatians 3:28 means there are to be no differences between men and women, because in other passages he clearly says there are to be differences (e.g. Eph 5:22-33; Col 3:18-19; 1 Cor 11:3-16, 14:33b-35; 1 Tim 2:8-15; Titus 2:2-6).

---

2   We are personally either sons or daughters—children—of God (Rom 8:16-17), but our filial relationship with the Father is established in the *Son*, and we receive the Spirit of the *Son* (Gal 4:1-7). So it is right to say "we are all equally sons of God", as women also receive the privileges and inheritance of a 'son'.

And so the male-female pair in Galatians 3:28 is actually different from the slave-free pair. While the New Testament gives instructions to slaves about how they are to conduct themselves in order to commend the gospel, the institution of slavery itself is never defended, neither is it explained with reference to God's intentions in creation or relations in the Godhead. Indeed, a slave is encouraged to gain their freedom if the opportunity to do so arises (1 Cor 7:21). Slavery was a cultural convention that rightly has ceased in most places around the world. The convention-confounding truth of Galatians 3:28 is that within the body of Christ, all those "in Christ Jesus" are *one*. The social and religious walls that previously kept people apart came tumbling down on the cross (cf. Eph 2:14-19).

Another way to relativise 1 Corinthians 14 so it does not apply to us is to blame a particular problem in Corinth for verses 33b-35 and then say that Paul's instructions applied only to that situation. These verses are then like medicine prescribed for an illness we don't have and can't get.

This sort of argument goes like this: Paul gave these instructions because the women in Corinth were chatterboxes or uneducated or were being disruptive and shouting across the building, and since we do not have that problem this passage is irrelevant to us.

But be warned! This is a dangerous way to read God's word—not least because it is impossible for us to be certain exactly what was happening in Corinth. To override the plain teaching of the Bible on the basis of a *possible* reconstruction is really taking matters into our own hands (especially when the text itself is silent on the circumstances that brought forth Paul's instructions).

Besides, there are several indications in the text that Paul's advice applies not just to a particular situation in Corinth but across the board. For starters, verse 33 says that this is the norm "in all the churches of the saints", as does verse 36, where Paul's rhetorical questions expose the Corinthians' penchant for heading off in their own direction on this matter.

And of course there is the fact that Paul finishes off this section by saying, "If anyone thinks that he is a prophet, or spiritual, he should acknowledge that the things I am writing to you are a matter of opinion..." No! "...are *a command of the Lord*" (v. 37)! Clearly in Paul's mind there is no room for disagreement.

Despite the way it might offend our modern sensibilities, there is no easy way of avoiding verses 33a-35. So let us take a closer look at them.

A closer look

From the beginning of chapter 12, Paul has been looking at the gifts that God gives to each believer for the benefit of all, for the common good (1 Cor 12:7). They are not gifts to be used by a person for that person's benefit. They are to be used in a way that benefits everyone. They are not like those gifts that children rip open on Christmas Day and think they have the exclusive right to use however and wherever they choose (including during church and Christmas lunch!). No, the gifts are not our possession to do with what we want.

All gifts, Paul insists, are to be exercised in a way that benefits *everyone*—believers and unbelievers alike. They are not to be used selfishly or without regard for other people. That is the point of chapter 13 (that famous wedding chapter) when it says:

> If I speak in the tongues of men and of angels, but have
> not love, I am a noisy gong or a clanging cymbal. And if
> I have prophetic powers, and understand all mysteries
> and all knowledge, and if I have all faith, so as to remove
> mountains, but have not love, I am nothing. (13:1-2)

You see, it is possible to be the most extraordinarily gifted person and yet in the exercise of those gifts actually to be nothing. It is possible to lose the blessing of those gifts, for yourself and others, by the way you use them.

The various gifts God gives us by his Spirit are to be used with love, and so they must be used to build the church (14:3-5, 12, 26). And if the gift is a 'speaking' gift then what is spoken must be intelligible (vv. 9-17).

So even though a person may be able to speak in tongues, unless those tongues can be and are interpreted so everyone can understand what is being said, it is better not to speak in tongues in church. As Paul says, "I thank God that I speak in tongues more than all of you. Nevertheless, in church I would rather speak five words with my mind in order to instruct others, than ten thousand words in a tongue" (vv. 18-19; cf. vv. 23-25). Love requires intelligibility.

But it also requires order, as verses 26-40 now tell us. What we find here—which was probably a bit of a surprise to the Corinthians and is to some of us—is that the ability to do something does not guarantee us the right to do it or that we will do it right.

Although *each* believer has received a gift through the Holy Spirit (12:4-7) and when believers come together "*each one* has a hymn, a lesson, a revelation, a tongue, or an interpretation" (14:26), *all of these* must be done in such a way that the church grows, numerically and in maturity, as it hears the reiteration and application of gospel truths.

And as you will know if you have ever been in a room full of people, this will mean that some people will have to remain silent.

1. Who is to keep silent?

Several Bible translations let us down here when it comes to the question of who is to remain silent, because it looks as though it is only women who are told to be silent. It looks like the women are the only ones who cop it!

But there are actually three groups of people who are told to be silent, and the same Greek word for 'silent' (*sigaō*) is used for each. There are tongue-speakers who are to be silent (v. 28), prophets who are to be silent (v. 30), and women who are to be silent (v. 34).

But how do we make sense of this? Paul has just said "each one" will have something to say, and now he is saying almost everyone is to be silent! Which is it—is it all in or all out? Well, it is both! Everyone will have something to contribute but not always.

There are certain times when certain people are to be silent.

The first group is those who speak in a tongue. Just because a person can speak in a tongue does not mean they can or should do it all the time. Paul gives three conditions for tongue-speakers in order to allow optimal building of the Christian community. When one tongue-speaker is speaking, the others are to be silent. When two or at the most three tongue-speakers have spoken, the rest are to remain silent. And most especially, if there is no interpreter then a tongue-speaker is to be silent.

Let me say in passing that Paul's instructions here are a far cry from what happens in many charismatic and Pentecostal churches. From my experience of visiting such churches and belonging to one of Sydney's largest Pentecostal churches for several years, it seems what most often happens is that everyone speaks in tongues all at once, hardly anyone interprets, and the whole thing is helped along by lots of clapping and loud music. Intelligibility and order are the last things on anyone's mind (cf. v. 14)!

But what Paul wants is intelligible order, not loud babble—however exhilarating. He wants what is being said to be clear so that everyone can learn from it. If that can't happen, says Paul, it is better to be silent.

Then he moves to the prophets.

Now although Paul is more enthusiastic about prophecy than tongues, both in verses 26-40 and in 1 Corinthians 14 generally, even prophets are told to be silent.

When are they to be silent? For starters, two or three prophets are to speak and others are to weigh what is said, and if a revelation comes to a prophet when another is speaking, the first speaker has to be silent. Presumably, too, once two or three have spoken then any other potential prophets are also to be silent.

There is no sense in which either the prophet or the tongue-speaker can blame the Holy Spirit for sweeping them off their feet and making them run off at the mouth. The gifts may be a manifestation of God's Spirit, but the person is responsible for using the gift wisely.

The tongue-speaker is perfectly able to wait their turn (v. 27) and, in fact, not speak in tongues at all in church and instead speak privately to God (v. 28). The prophet is perfectly able to wait his or her turn (v. 31) and sit down if they are interrupted (v. 30) because the spirits of the prophets are subject to the prophets (v. 32).

And why is this so? It is because "God is not a God of confusion but of peace" (v. 33). In fact, right from the opening verses of Genesis, where the earth was a chaotic darkness and God divided light from dark and made order from chaos, it is clear that God is a God of order and peace.

That does not mean that our church services should be deadly boring. It is a terrible indictment against us if they are! How could meeting as the body of Christ in the presence of the living God to hear his word and glorify him ever be boring?

What it does mean is that God's own character is to shape our participation and use of the gifts he gives. He is a God of order and a God of peace. He is a God who speaks to his people intelligibly (cf. vv. 21-22). He is a God of love. This means that those who participate must do so in the right ways, where love governs everything and sometimes requires a would-be tongue-speaker or prophet to be silent.

Which brings us to the women in verses 34-35, who *all* seem to be told to be silent *all* of the time.

As we have already seen, the Greek here presents us with a challenge. The same Greek word means both 'woman' and 'wife' (*gunē*) and the same Greek word can mean both 'man' and 'husband' (*anēr*). Does it mean here that only wives are to be silent or that all the women generally are to be silent?

It might be that Paul primarily has married women in mind here. I say "might be" and "primarily" because of verse 35, which tells women to ask *their own* men at home. I assume it is this ambiguity the ESV is trying to capture when it uses 'women' and not 'wives' throughout, but 'husbands' rather than 'men'.

But the Greek could just as easily mean they should ask their own *men* at home, which—given that households in the first century had a well-established pattern of male leadership—could simply mean, "Women, when you get home ask the head of the house".

Moreover, in the ancient world, not only did most women marry at a young age, but also married women had greater freedom and social status than unmarried women. So it is unlikely that with so little explanation Paul would casually overturn that convention by giving unmarried women more freedom than wives.

So the answer to "Which women?" is probably "All women".

2. When are they to keep silent?

As we saw when we first looked at these verses, Paul seems to say that women should be silent in church, full stop. End of discussion. No exceptions allowed. Indeed, there are some churches today that take these verses just this way. Women are not allowed to read the Bible in church or say the prayers or lead the singing or liturgy, and they are not allowed in the pulpit. They are silent with a capital S!

But the problem with this is that it goes beyond what we find in the New Testament. Sure enough, 1 Timothy 2 says women are to be quietly submissive, which means not teaching or having governing authority over men, but it does not say women are *never* to address the church—whether or not men are there.

And from 1 Corinthians 14 we only have to flip back a couple of pages to chapter 11 to see that Paul has no objections to women praying and prophesying in the Christian assembly provided they do so in a gender-appropriate way. It is clearly okay for women to speak in church at least *sometimes*. Hence, churches that prevent women from ever speaking have taken 1 Corinthians 14 too far.

However, there is a time when women are not to speak. When is it?

One suggestion has been that Paul is objecting to women babbling on in tongues and that this is evident in his choice of words (*laleō*), where he does not use the usual Greek verb for the speaking that women are not to do (*legō*). But even a quick look at the words that Paul uses in chapter 14 is enough to show that this linguistic distinction just does not hold, since he uses both of these Greek verbs for tongues and for intelligible speech.

So when are the women not to speak? They are not to speak while "the others", that is, the congregation, are weighing the prophecies (v. 29).

If we take verse 29 as an introductory or summary verse regulating the practice of prophecy—in a similar way that verses 27-28 regulated the practice of tongues—we find the verse has two parts. The first part says, "Let two or three prophets speak" and then how this is meant to work is explained in verses 30-32.

The second part of verse 29 then says, "and let the others weigh what is said". As we saw in our discussion of prophecy in the previous chapter, not everything said in the name of prophecy is actually from God. Prophecies cannot be accepted uncritically. We find similar statements elsewhere (1 Thess 5:19-21; 1 John 4:1-6). Prophecy has to be sifted and evaluated and tested. It has to be rubber-stamped, and only when it has been approved and accepted does it have authority in the church.

And it is this evaluation process mentioned in 1 Corinthians 14:29b that Paul returns to in verses 33b-38: first, in regards to the involvement of women in the public activity of weighing (vv. 33b-35); and then, in regards to criteria that tested the authenticity of the prophets themselves (vv. 37-38). Just as Paul has given tongue-speakers and prophets instructions about who may speak and when and how they may speak, he gives instructions about who may weigh prophecy and when and how they are to do so. And part of this is that women are not to speak during this process.

So although the women might well have their own opinions about whether or not a prophecy is the real thing, they are not to participate during the weighing.

And, when you think about it, this is not too different from a tongue-speaker who might have a tongue to speak but who has to be silent because there is no interpreter; and the prophet who might have a revelation but who is interrupted by another prophet.

Paul's instruction is not a comment on the *value* of what would be said; he is just saying that for the sake of order and (in this case) the relationship between men and women, the women are not to speak.

3. Why are they to keep silent?

So we have worked out *when* women are to be silent. What about *why*? How can we be sure it is not just a cultural thing? Well, fortunately the passage gives us a stack of reasons and that is not one of them.

There are (as I count them) at least six reasons. Some of them apply to the passage as a whole, and some just to the instructions for women:

(i) As we have seen, God is a God of order (v. 33a). That is, the God who created order out of chaos and light out of darkness is the same God who desires order and peace among his people. He did not create us for chaos, but for relationships of order and peace.

(ii) Paul's advice concerning women reflects the universal practice of churches (vv. 33b, 36). He is not demanding anything more of the Corinthian women than is demanded of God's people in all the churches. This repeats a point Paul has made already in this letter: there is to be uniformity amongst the churches, and gospel faithfulness demands that the Corinthians conduct themselves as other believers do (4:17, 7:17, 11:16). While every Christian community will have certain differences, there are some aspects of community life that are non-negotiable and shared amongst all churches.

(iii) Paul's main reason seems to be that this is what "the Law" says (14:34). But what law?

Earlier in the chapter, Paul introduces a quote from Isaiah by saying it comes from "the Law" (v. 21). However, strictly speaking, it does not come from those books in the Old Testament that deal with the Law,[3] but from a prophetic book. He seems to be using the term 'the Law' as shorthand for the whole Old Testament. So it is reasonable to assume that he has the Old Testament in mind here as well.

But why doesn't he tell us exactly which part of the Old Testament? Well, possibly because he has just written chapter 11 where it is clear that Genesis 1 and 2 are on view. It is the same here. It is not that Paul has one particular verse in mind, but the whole pattern of relationships that is established in the garden of Eden.

Our study of 1 Timothy 2 and 1 Corinthians 11 has already taken us to these early pages of the Bible, on which Paul bases a major reason for his teaching about the

---

3   i.e. Genesis, Exodus, Leviticus, Numbers and Deuteronomy

pattern of relationships between men and women in church. Genesis 1 tells us that God made men and women equally in his image with equal dignity and common purpose, and Genesis 2 tells us that even though both are made in God's image, the man was made first and the woman was made as "a helper fit for him" (Gen 2:18).

That is, although they were both to "fill the earth and subdue it" (Gen 1:28), the man was to do that by leading and the woman was to do that by helping. This fits well with the statement in 1 Corinthians 14:34 that women are to "be in submission, *as the Law also says*". Furthermore, as Paul explicitly revisits these foundational chapters in Genesis to explain the ordered relationship and different responsibilities of husbands and wives (Eph 5:22-33), it seems reasonable that he would point to the same source here in 1 Corinthians 14.

The evaluation of prophecies was an authoritative activity that determined what was to be learned by the congregation from the prophecies people shared. While women were able to prophesy, they were not to take part in this authoritative activity but were to be in submission—by not asking questions and by keeping silent as the weighing process occurred.

(iv) I take it that this is what lies behind the fourth reason Paul gives, which is that "it is shameful for a woman to speak in church" (v. 35). It is shameful, I assume, in the same way that it is shameful for a woman to wear her hair like a man's or for a man to wear his hair like a woman's (11:6, 14). It is conduct that undermines or denies God-given gender differences and so reflects badly on everyone.

(v) Paul's fifth reason is that these are not his ideas but "a command of the Lord" (v. 37), and that accepting this teaching is another test of a true prophet. Both in the first century and for us today, it is impossible to be truly spiritual and disagree with the Lord's apostle, because as the Lord's apostle Paul is an inspired faithful messenger of God's truth (4:1). Those who do not recognize this do not deserve to be recognized—then *and* now. They have disqualified themselves.

(vi) Which brings us to the last reason Paul gives, which is that when we come together everything is to be done "decently and in order" (v. 40). That's what love means. Love means that we have the interest of everybody at heart, and that what takes place is orderly and intelligible and does not deny the ordered differences between women and men.

Which right is right?

So does 1 Corinthians 14 have any meaning for us today? Is it relevant? Has it passed its use-by date?

No, its shelf life has not expired. This chapter is simply building on what we saw in chapter 11, where Paul went right back to the garden of Eden to explain the pattern of relationships between men and women. You will remember too that in the earlier text he also gave the relationships in the Godhead as an enduring 'transcultural' reason for male headship.

As uncomfortable as 1 Corinthians 14:33b-35 might be for us, we cannot dismiss it as a cultural oddity, because the reasons Paul gives for it are not *cultural* reasons. It is not like the old-fashioned Victorian rules that the people in the TV program had to obey. Paul's reasons cut to the very heart of who God is, how he made us, and who he made us to be.

So what does this text mean for us?

My hunch is that it may not apply directly to many of us. Sadly, in my opinion, few evangelical churches practise anything close to what could be called congregational prophecy, and unless we go to a church that has people prophesying *and* then tests those prophecies, women may never have to be silent when prophecies are being weighed.

I have only once been to a church where prophecies were given and then weighed. It was the same church I mentioned in the previous chapter regarding headscarves. What happened was that we were told an opportunity to share prophecies was approaching, and anyone who believed they had a revelation was first to go to the elders gathered at the front so the elders could weigh the message before it was spoken to the church.

Admittedly this is slightly different from what we see in 1 Corinthians 14, but at least it provided an opportunity for people other than the appointed male teachers to contribute to the public gathering, *and* it sought to ensure some 'quality control' over what was spoken. My observation is that churches often miss out on both of these!

Where 1 Corinthians 14 does perhaps touch on current evangelical church life is during the question times that can follow sermons in church or talks at university campus meetings and church fellowship conferences and retreats.

It is possible—and I suspect many of us have seen it happen—for a woman to ask a question of a male preacher in such a way that it sounds as though (or in reality) she is weighing or challenging what he has said, and not really asking a question at all.

Now, I am not convinced this text tells us that women cannot ask questions at all in those contexts, but it does say: be careful how you ask them. Do not let your manner lack an attitude of submission. Now, of course, if all believers are to submit to those over us in the Lord then men have to watch how they ask questions too, but for women this means that we are to ask our questions in a way that is respectfully feminine and quietly submissive—notwithstanding the fact that our questions are hopefully intelligent, thoughtful and thought-provoking!

In addition to this, there are several other important applications of this part of Paul's letter to the Corinthians.

One of the obvious implications of the wider passage of 1 Corinthians 14:26-40 is that the ability to do something does not come with the right to do it.

It is not good enough to say, "Because I can play the piano I have a right to play in the band", or "Because I led a Bible study group last year, I have a right to lead one this year", or "Because I am a good Bible teacher I have a right to preach". Or to put it in the way it is often expressed, and where it is not about *self*-promotion: because a particular woman is a gifted Bible teacher she should be allowed to preach in church.

The *ability* to do something does not come with the *right* to do it. This is because there are greater issues at stake. What is best for the congregation? What promotes order? What does God's word say about the relationships between men and women?

And because of these issues, it might be that even though we are capable of doing something, the right thing might be not to do it. It is interesting that in 1 Corinthians 14 there is no suggestion that those tongue-speakers or prophets who are to be silent have second-rate messages. It is just not the time for them to speak. In fact, Paul is more concerned about order and intelligibility than that these messages be spoken.

A second take-home lesson from this wider text is the importance of our contributions in church being for the benefit *of the whole*. All the gifts in the world and all the Bible knowledge in the world are of no benefit if love is not the governing factor. When we participate, we participate for the sake of others (and for the glory of God), not ourselves.

And that means there is no place for envy. We cannot look

at someone doing something and think, "That's not fair; why can't I do that?" because that would be to come at things from completely the wrong angle. The church family is not there so that we can have a platform on which to perform. Our focus should be on what is good for the whole, and the guidelines Paul gives us here are intelligibility and order as a means of expressing love and conforming to the character of God.

Finally, and more broadly, these verses about the participation of women in church show us that 1 Timothy 2 is not one isolated text that needs to be taken with a grain of salt because it contradicts the rest of the New Testament, as is sometimes claimed. Rather—as we should expect of the divinely-inspired word of God—1 Timothy 2, 1 Corinthians 11 and 14, and Galatians 3 all give a consistent picture of the relationships between men and women and the implications of that for church life in the first century and today.

And so seeking to obey these things today is not like being the people on the TV show who stepped back into Victorian England for three months and tried to live by outdated and outmoded rules and conventions that benefitted no-one.

God communicates clearly in his word, which contains all we need to know in order to please him. Indeed, Scripture lays before us the way of blessing and of curse, and presents us with a choice about which way we will chose. The three passages we have looked at that deal with gender relationships when the church gathers are no different. God wrote them for our good, and obedience to them will both please him and bring blessing to us.

For these reasons, and despite the climate of our times, we only stand to benefit if we practise what his word commands— being careful not to add or take away from it.

PART II | WITHIN THE HOME

5 | THE DIVINE MARRIAGE: EPHESIANS 5

I THINK IT IS FAIR TO ASSUME that everyone reading this book has had some experience of weddings. Whether it was our own wedding, a family member's, a friend's, a workmate's, or just a wedding we have seen at the movies, all of us have some exposure to weddings. We know what happens.

Let me narrow that down a little. I suspect it is also fair to assume that most of us have been to a Christian wedding—perhaps many Christian weddings! In fact, even if we're not clergy or marriage celebrants, I suspect many of us have spent enough sunny Saturdays inside cold church buildings at weddings that we could recite the marriage vows, if not the entire service, off by heart.

And that shows what we're up against when we come to Ephesians 5. Because in one way or another, through songs, Bible readings, sermons, liturgy and vows, at many of those weddings we would have come across Ephesians 5 or some echo of it.

My guess is that many of us have also heard sermons on this text as part of the regular preaching program in our churches. Ephesians is a popular New Testament letter, and this is a popular text. What preacher doesn't want to tell the flock that Christ loved the church and gave himself up for her?

But there is a danger in all this exposure, which is that familiarity breeds contempt. The passage can sound so familiar that our brains switch off. It's a case of "Yeah, yeah, now tell me something I don't know".

Of course, the other challenge is that all of us come to this passage with firsthand experience of marriage. Whether or not we are married ourselves, most of us grew up in families, so we have a lifetime's exposure to the ups and downs of married life this side of the Fall. We know that however good the wedding photos are, the day-to-day, year-to-year, decade-to-decade realities are very different. Perhaps that is why weddings are such an emotional roller-coaster—for the couple, the parents, everyone. We want to accentuate the positive and eliminate the negative (it *is* a wedding after all!), but we know that 'till death do us part' and 'for better or for worse' are promises that can sound romantic when things are going well, and like life sentences when things are not.

So that's the challenge for us as we turn to Ephesians 5:21-33: to put aside our familiarity and take a fresh look at this part of God's word, and to do it outside of a wedding service and away from the shadow of our own experiences.

But before we do that, here is a very potted summary of what we have covered so far.

We have looked at 1 Timothy 2 and 1 Corinthians 11 and 14 and seen clearly that men and women are equally saved, equally loved and equally valued members in Christ's church. We have also seen that this equality does not deny the fact that when we come together in church, God wants women and men to make different contributions.

And although it might be convenient for us to decide that the idea of an ordered pattern of gender relationships no longer applies to us because it is at odds with our times, we have seen that this option is not open to us. The fact that Paul explains this teaching as he does—from God's creation purposes and human beginnings before and after the Fall (Genesis 1-3), and from relations within the Godhead (1 Cor 11:3)—means that the Bible's teaching of gender equality and difference is something we need to hear and put into practice in our own cultural context.

At first glance

We will begin by placing our text in context within Ephesians 5:

> [18]And do not get drunk with wine, for that is debauchery, but be filled with the Spirit, [19]addressing one another in psalms and hymns and spiritual songs, singing and making melody to the Lord with your heart, [20]giving thanks always and for everything to God the Father in the name of our Lord Jesus Christ, [21]submitting to one another out of reverence for Christ.
>
> [22]Wives, submit to your own husbands, as to the Lord. [23]For the husband is the head of the wife even as Christ is the head of the church, his body, and is himself its Saviour. [24]Now as the church submits to Christ, so also wives should submit in everything to their husbands.
>
> [25]Husbands, love your wives, as Christ loved the church and gave himself up for her, [26]that he might sanctify her, having cleansed her by the washing of water with the word, [27]so that he might present the church to himself in splendour, without spot or wrinkle or any such thing, that she might be holy and without blemish. [28]In the same way husbands should love their wives as their own bodies. He who loves his wife loves himself. [29]For no-one ever hated his own flesh, but nourishes and cherishes it, just as Christ does the church, [30]because we are members of his body. [31]"Therefore a man shall leave his father and mother and hold fast to his wife, and the

two shall become one flesh." [32] This mystery is profound, and I am saying that it refers to Christ and the church. [33] However, let each one of you love his wife as himself, and let the wife see that she respects her husband.

(EPH 5:18-33)

As I have already mentioned, people often claim that the passages dealing with gender in the New Testament are old and complicated and we cannot be sure what they mean. But we have found that this is not actually the case when it comes to 1 Timothy 2 and 1 Corinthians 11 and 14. So, as we have done previously, we will begin by making some fairly straightforward observations.

The first thing to notice is that this text is clearly about husbands and wives.

With the texts we have looked at previously, because of the original Bible language, we have had to work out if they are talking about men and women generally or husbands and wives specifically. But here in Ephesians 5 this question is easily settled. It is husbands and wives on view, not men and women generally. Three things tell us this beyond a doubt:

(i) Paul's quote from Genesis 2:24 is unambiguously about the institution and rationale of the first marriage (v. 31).

(ii) The section about husbands and wives is part of a larger section dealing with three sets of household relationships: verses 22-33 address the marriage relationship, 6:1-4 addresses children and parents, and 6:5-9 addresses slaves and masters. Also, unlike the other passages we have looked at so far, these instructions are not set within the context of church.

(iii) You will notice that wives are told to submit to *their own* husbands (v. 22). It does not say "to *every* man/husband" or even "to *a* man/husband". Husbands, similarly, are to love *their own* wives as themselves. These are relationship specific commands: wives are to submit in the way envisaged in this text only to their own husbands, not to *all* men; and husbands are to love their own wives, not *all* women!

So, even at first glance, we know that if we are married, this passage applies to us in a way that it doesn't to those who are not married. That does not mean that we can skip over this bit in our Bibles if we are not married; God alone knows our end from the beginning. But if we are married then this one is particularly for us, so sit up and take notice!

The second thing to note is that this text is not just about a cultural expression of marriage. Paul is not saying, "This is how marriage is in the first century, but if the culture changes then it might no longer apply".

There is no denying that cultural expressions of marriage do change. These days, it is a brave (or foolish?) husband who doesn't pull his weight in the kitchen or know how to change a dirty nappy or iron a shirt. But Paul is not talking about a cultural practice that belonged only in the first century.

Paul expects what he is saying to be relevant as long as there are men and women being joined in marriage. We can know this because, as he does in most of the New Testament passages about gender relations, Paul goes right back to God's original intentions for women and men in Genesis to support what he is saying. That is why he quotes Genesis 2:24.

But this Ephesians passage gives an additional reason for not dismissing this teaching as purely cultural, and that is the fact that Paul bases what he is saying on the relationship of Christ and the church. In fact, the relationship of Christ and the church provides the bedrock for what Paul says to husbands and wives—and that relationship is bigger, better and more permanent than *any* cultural expression of marriage.

So because Paul talks about Christ's relationship to the church, this passage is for us *all*—whether we are single, widowed, married, divorced, whatever. If we are Christians then we are members of Christ's church and this text therefore has something to say to us, because it tells us about Christ's love for us *all*.

The controlling theme: Christ and the church

As we've heard Ephesians 5 read out at weddings, we might have missed the fact that there is more in this passage about the relationship of Christ and the church than there is about earthly marriage. Of the 200-odd words between verses 22 and 33, more than half deal directly with Christ and the church.

The relationship of Christ and the church provides the structure for all that Paul wants to say to wives and husbands. You will see that comparative terms like 'as', 'just as' and 'in the same way' run right through the text. Paul is asking wives and husbands to be *like* something, to resemble something. He is holding up a model and telling them to "be like *this*". And the model is Christ and the church.

So what do we learn about Christ and the church?

We learn three things: we learn that Christ is the head of the church; that the church submits to her head; and that Christ loves the church.

1. Christ is the head of the church

Let's start with Christ as the head of the church. Paul has already used this description twice for the Lord Jesus (1:22, 4:15; cf. 1:10). In both those texts the role of Christ as head is a reference to his rule and authority, even when his nourishing of the church is also on view as it is in Ephesians 4:16 and in the text before us now (5:29-30).

In light of these earlier references, Paul begins by simply reiterating this profound theological truth: "Christ is the head of the church, his body, and is himself its Saviour" (v. 23). He then explains the consequence of this headship for the church, which is that "the church submits to Christ" (v. 24). But *how* does the church submit to Christ?

2. The church submits to her head

I heard once about an adult Bible study group that was studying this passage and discussing the concept of 'submission'. In the course of the discussion, a man who was a new Christian asked if 'submission' meant the same thing in Ephesians 5 as it did in the only other context in which he had encountered this word—in wrestling, where the loser signals his defeat by hitting the canvas and saying, "I submit!" in order to avoid further humiliation and pain.

It is an understandable question—and good on him for asking it! After all, 'submission' is not a common word these days, and it is easy for us to look at this common New Testament theme through modern lenses that distort the intended meaning. But this wrestling analogy is definitely *not* what is on view in Ephesians 5.

It is true that the spiritual powers and rival authorities over which Christ has been appointed head may not have submitted (or will not eventually submit) *willingly* (1:19-22). But the church's submission to Christ is a joyful, wholehearted, willing and voluntary submission. There is no sense in Ephesians generally or here in chapter 5 that submission to Christ is forced upon the church against her will.

The church is not *made* to submit. Rather, the church *chooses* to submit herself to the rule of her Saviour, Christ—and not just in some things but in everything.

It's worth asking if that is how we view our submission to Christ. Does the rule of Christ extend happily into every corner of our lives? Paul has no doubt that the church submits to the authority of Christ totally, happily and in absolutely everything! There is no 'sometimes' or 'grudgingly' or 'possibly' in his statement. Could we say the same about our churches, I wonder? Could we say the same about ourselves? Of course, it should be obvious that Paul is not talking here about the *institutional* churches that make the headlines (usually for all the wrong reasons). He is talking about the true church, the spiritual church to which we belong if Jesus is our Saviour and Lord, and which joyfully and willingly always submits to him in everything.

The earlier chapters of Ephesians help fill out the picture of this relationship of headship and submission even more.

For his part, Christ is the cornerstone of the new temple into which we are being built (2:19-21). He dwells and rules in our hearts by faith (3:17). His love surpasses knowledge but as his people we can know it (3:18-19). He loved us and gave himself up for us (5:2). He gives the church all it needs to grow and to please him (4:11-16). Indeed, the very existence of the church is due to the work of God in Christ, and our union with him (1:4-13, 2:4-7, 3:10-12, etc.).

For our part, we can only approach God in and through Christ (2:13). When we 'learn Christ', he changes us (4:20). His sacrificial love is to be the model for our obedience (5:2) and as Christians we are to find out what pleases him and do it (5:10). We are to understand his will (5:17) and be filled by his Spirit, joining together to sing his praises (5:18-19).

That is the picture Paul gives of the church submitting to Christ. It is submission that benefits Christ inasmuch as it gives him the reverence and obedience due to him as Saviour and Lord. Yet, at the same time and perhaps counter-intuitively, it is submission that always benefits us, because Christ the head loves his bride, the church.

3. Christ loves the church

And what shockingly self-sacrificial love it is! "Christ loved the church and gave himself up for her" in order to sanctify and cleanse her (vv. 25-26), and to present her to himself as a radiant bride, and to make her "holy and without blemish" (v. 27). His loving headship is all in her favour. His self-sacrifice was about making the unlovable lovable.

That is what Christ has done for *us all*, individually and collectively, if we belong to him. We have been washed and cleansed, transformed and adorned by him.

In our cleanliness-obsessed and disinfected society, it is hard for us to appreciate the amazing transformation this involves. But if we look at the marriage imagery in Ezekiel 16:1-14 that seems to have been in the back of Paul's mind, we see that Jesus Christ has taken a filthy, naked, shameful social outcast, and washed her and clothed her and taken her as his cherished bride.

When I worked as a nurse at an inner-city hospital, occasionally the ambulances would bring in homeless women. I know it is a tragic thing to say, but you could smell the street on these women before you pulled back the curtain to go in to their bedside. Years of dirt and dead skin and body odour and infestations had built up. Their eyes were darkened. Their faces were shrouded with unkempt hair. Their clothes were torn. Most people who saw them would have turned and looked away.

But while these women were in hospital, they were cared for and well-fed. They were washed and given clothes. Their nails were cleaned and cut, their hair brushed, their teeth cleaned. The transformation was amazing.

That is like the transformation Christ has wrought in us, his bride. We are chosen by Christ, washed by him, joined to him, cherished by him. We are no longer guilty, despised, morally filthy and ashamed. And of course it is a far greater transformation than the difference between a homeless woman and a bridal magazine cover girl.

Christ *has done* this. He has washed us and in doing so has made us his bride. And that washing came to us through the powerful word of the gospel (Eph 5:26). Our bridegroom and head of the church has cleansed us and changed us and adorned us as his bride (Rev 19:7; 21:2, 9).

So this passage shows us the dizzy heights of Christ's love for his bride. We have spent some time exploring this controlling theme of Christ and the church not only because of its own merit, but also because Paul uses it as the theological basis for his instructions about the comparatively mundane relationships of our homes.

So what does this passage say to Christian wives and husbands?

The 'like' theme: wives and husbands

The first thing to notice is that Paul gives much shorter instructions to wives than those he gives to husbands (which might be a relief for the wives!). The second thing to notice is that Paul starts by addressing the wives, then he addresses the husbands, and then he finishes the section by returning to the wives.

This tells us that Paul considers wives to be morally responsible agents, participants with equal dignity and membership in Christ's church and in marriage, with real choice and responsibility. Neither the husband nor the wife has any less choice or moral agency than the other.

Notice too that Paul does not speak to the husbands about their wives' behaviour, and he does not tell husbands to make their wives submit.[1] Rather, he goes straight to the wives and instructs them how to relate to their husbands. Similarly, he goes straight to the husbands and tells them how to relate to their wives. Each is answerable for his or her own conduct. There is no sense that either is to force or manipulate compliance from the other.

---

1   Nor does he tell wives to make their husbands lead or tell their husbands how to lead!

1. Wives: reasons and response

Wives are to submit themselves to their husbands (v. 22), or as Paul puts it at the end of the passage, they are to fear or respect their husbands (v. 33).

And why are they to do that?

The reason for a wife's submission to her husband, put simply, is that he is her head. The logic goes like this: the husband is head of the wife as Christ is head of the church, and so the wife is to submit to her husband as the church submits to Christ (vv. 23-24). There is a parallelism between the two pairs.

Now clearly the husband is not head of his wife in all the ways that Christ is head of the church. But there are enough similarities between the headship of husbands and that of Christ that Paul makes this statement about the husband's headship in verse 23 without any further qualification.

When we looked at 1 Corinthians 11, we saw that male headship first found expression in God's creation of man and woman, recorded in Genesis 1 and 2, when woman was made *from* man and *for* man. From these human beginnings, and from the relationships within the Godhead, Paul concluded that there is a God-given pattern of relationships between women and men that is to be expressed *in the church*. We also saw this pattern in 1 Corinthians 14 and 1 Timothy 2, although not with explicit reference to male headship but rather in 'submission' language. Here in Ephesians, gender roles and responsibilities *in marriage* are also based on God's creation purposes, as the reference to Genesis 2:24 makes plain (vv. 29-31).

But in Ephesians 5, we also see that the blueprint for human marriage is in fact the relationship of Christ and the church, and so the ordered relationship of husbands and wives is defined by the relationship of Christ and the church. This means the wife is to be like the church, and the husband is to be like Christ. The two are parallel.

And because of that parallel, the wife's response to the headship of her husband (v. 22) is to be the same as the church's response to Christ: she is to submit herself to him by willingly recognizing and accepting his authority—in everything (v. 24).

Now, my guess is that while we may have had difficulties with the previous texts, this statement might take our objections to a whole new level. Not only does this text apply directly to many of us (rather than only to those women who want identical ministries to men), but also there is something wildly counter-cultural about this statement.

I mean, who submits to *anyone* these days? And in *everything*? All of us, women and men, are children of the Enlightenment who think of ourselves as autonomous self-determining individuals. And that's even before we factor in the more modern concerns of gender and power.

I have actually heard women and men groan or cry out in objection and shock when this passage has been read at weddings—and not just the *non*-Christian guests. Somehow, the wife's submission is more shocking to them than the high bar set for husbands!

Our society has moved a long way from this biblical ideal of marriage. Many of our churches have even moved a long way from it—so much so that it may be a new idea for some of us. For others it may be old territory, part of God's word that has been like a pebble in our shoe for years. We would like to get rid of it but we know we can't treat God's word like that.

But this is God's word and, as his people, we need to hear his voice and pray that he will give us the will to obey it. God says to us here that wives are willingly to recognize and accept their husbands' headship every day and in everything.

This is fleshed out at the end of the passage, where Paul uses a word related to the one he first used when he introduced the idea of submission (*phobeō*). In the first instance, we are told to submit "to one another out of *reverence* for Christ" (v. 21). In the last verse, a wife is to *respect* or *fear* her husband (v. 33). The repetition of this word is yet another indication of the parallel that exists between the two pairs of relationships. The wife is to submit to her husband *as* the church does to Christ.

2. Husbands: reasons and response

These parallels continue in the two reasons Paul gives husbands for his charge to them, both of which flow out of the husband's headship.

The first reason is that as head, the husband is to be *like Christ*. It is a simple matter of identity. In the same way that the wife has responsibilities that arise simply because of her identity with the church—she is to be *like the church*—so too the husband has responsibilities that arise simply because his headship reflects the headship of Christ (v. 25).

The second reason is that husbands are to "love their wives *as their own bodies*" (vv. 28-29). In God's good purposes, when a man and woman marry, the two become one flesh, one entity. So for a husband to care for his wife is really also for him to care for himself! The welfare of the two cannot be separated. For a man to hate his wife or treat her poorly is not only going against the command to love as Christ loved; it is also for him to hate himself! So real is the unity between a husband and wife that when a husband loves and nurtures his wife, he is in fact loving himself (v. 28)! Her good is *his* good. He cannot separate his interests from hers, or hers from his.

So whereas we might have expected Paul to spell out the implications of a husband's headship by telling men to rule over their wives—given how common it is for those with authority to use it harshly for their own benefit rather than benevolently (cf. Mark 10:42)—what we find is that Paul tells husbands not to *rule* but rather to *love*. And he says it not just once but three times (Eph 5:25, 28, 33).

And the guidance Paul gives for how husbands are to love their wives (wives, take note) does not come from romantic movie heroes or from being compared to someone else's husband or from books on 'how to improve your marriage' left strategically open around the house. Husbands are to be guided by the love of Christ for the church, whose headship was established through that selfless love which caused him to give himself up to death for her sake.

Earthly husbands are to model themselves on *Christ's* sacrificial love. In the same way that Christ feeds the church and protects, cherishes, nurtures and cares for her, so *earthly* husbands are to love their wives. They are to do this both because this is the way that Christ loves the church, *and* because this is how they treat their own bodies—and in some sense their wives *are* their own bodies, since in marriage the two become one flesh (v. 31).

This last point explains why Paul finishes his discussion of the marriage relationship with a variation of the command in Leviticus 19:18 to "love your neighbour as yourself": "let each one of you love *his wife* as himself' (v. 33). If in marriage the two become one flesh, then loving your wife as yourself *is* loving yourself! Her good is also your good. There is no more intimate expression of loving your neighbour, since a man's wife is not only his closest neighbour but also his one flesh—in some sense his own body, as he also is hers.

Untying the knots

By now you will have noticed that the two relationships on view in this passage weave their way in and out, and most of the time it is clear which relationship is in the foreground: husbands and wives or Christ and the church. They are like two strands on a rope. But there are a few places where it is not immediately clear which one is on view. It's as if the two strands get stuck in a knot, and we have to spend some time loosening the knot so that we can work out which of the pairs is on view.

We find the first knot in the verses that talk about Christ as saviour (vv. 23, 25ff). At first glance, these verses might seem to say that the husband is the saviour of his wife as Christ is the Saviour of the church. In fact, someone said just this to me when I was newly engaged.

But it is clear in our English Bibles and even clearer in the original language that the description of Christ as the Saviour of his body applies only to Christ, and not to the husband (v. 23). Without getting too technical, the word order of the original puts the emphasis on Christ alone being the focus of the statement "his body, and is himself its Saviour". Also, the sentence immediately following begins with a 'but' (v. 24; "now" in the ESV). It is as if Paul is saying, "But now I want to return to what these pairs have in common rather than what distinguishes them: as the church submits to Christ, so also..." So Paul is basing his instructions to wives on the fact that the husband is the head of the wife, not because he is her saviour or because she is his body.

And what's more, what Paul has to say about the saving and cleansing work of Christ (vv. 25-26) clearly isn't a *literal* statement about how husbands are to love their wives (i.e. every husband must die so his wife can be forgiven). Rather, Paul means that Christ's love is a model for the husband's love, and that the goal of the husband's love for his wife is to be the same as the goal of Christ's love for the church.

The husband is to promote his wife's godliness and sanctification, sparing no effort in advancing the work of Christ in her life. He is to help her prepare for the future marriage of Christ and the church. In doing that, the husband is not his wife's saviour. The rest of the New Testament makes clear that Christ alone is our

Saviour, and there is only one mediator between God and men and women, the Lord Jesus Christ (e.g. John 14:6; 1 Tim 2:5-6). Rather, the husband is to love his wife with the same self-sacrificial love, purpose and goal that her Saviour does.

The second knot we need to untie occurs in the quote from Genesis 2:24 and in Paul's comment (Eph 5:31-32).

I take it that none of us is surprised to find this Genesis quote being used in a passage on human marriage. After all, in its original location in Genesis it explains the union of the first man and woman; it is used again in 1 Corinthians 6 to describe a casual sexual liaison with a prostitute; and it is used in the Anglican marriage service when the minister says, "'For this reason a man shall leave his father and mother and be joined to his wife, and the two shall become one.' So they are no longer two but one."

But its appearance in Ephesians 5:31 *should* surprise us because here Genesis 2:24 isn't primarily about a man and a woman—it is about Christ and the church.

One of my great passions is Michelangelo. So when I was backpacking through Europe many years ago, top on my list of 'must-sees' was of course Michelangelo's 'David'. But when I got to Florence I discovered there were Davids everywhere I looked. He was on postcards, in parks and plazas—even roadside stalls had Davids for sale. But I always knew when I saw them that I was looking at a copy (some of them very bad copies!). I knew that seeing them wasn't the same as seeing the real thing.

What Paul is saying in Ephesians 5 is that the relationship of Christ and the church is the real thing: that the two (i.e. Christ and the church) have become one flesh—we are members of his body (v. 30)—and that this mystery is profound because from this union of Christ and the church we can learn what Christian marriage is meant to look like.

Just as I would have been a fool to mistake the copies of

Michelangelo's 'David' for the real thing, so too *we* are fools if we think (in our marriage-rejecting-but-wedding-obsessed culture) that *earthly* marriage is the real thing. When I saw the real David, I knew I was looking at the real thing. It exceeded all my expectations. How much more should that be our experience when we consider the real marriage?

The real thing is Christ and the church—and the reality is that if we belong to Christ, all of us are part of that marriage.

Isn't that amazing? Have you ever sat in a wedding service or flipped through a bridal magazine and realized that the blueprint for marriage—the reason God fashioned marriage as he did—was to provide a beautiful earthly reflection of the eschatological love and union of his Son with those he died to save? Perhaps now you will!

The shape of submission

Having teased out those knots, it is now time to tease out the idea of submission. What is it? How do we put it into practice?

The remarkable thing is just how little information Paul gives about how it works out in practice. The questions we might ask (What *exactly* does submission involve? Can a wife correct her husband? Can she earn more than him? Can a woman with a strong personality marry a man who is less strong?) are not even on Paul's radar.

And that is a blessing! So often we want things spelled out in lists and rules, especially those of us who like measuring our spiritual progress by ticking boxes. But that is *one-size-fits-all holiness*, and fortunately God does not deal with us like that— because we are all different sizes!

Each one of us is unique and so every marriage is different, with different strengths and weaknesses, weathering different seasons of life with different demands and different stresses. In all these circumstances and through all these differences, Christ is working in each of us to make us holy, not with a one-size-fits-all approach but transforming us as individuals to be like him.

So what Paul gives us is not a step-by-step list of instructions on how to submit, but general parameters for wifely submission.

The first is that a wife is to submit to her husband "as to the Lord" (v. 22). This means that her submission to her husband is an expression of her obedience to the rule of Christ, and also that her submission is to be in keeping with her submission to her Lord. And because of that, we make a mistake if we think that a wife's submission is just about human relationships.

In reality, a wife's submission to her husband is part and parcel of her submission to Christ because, as Scripture tells us here, Christ requires it of her. This means that if a wife chooses continually to disregard or disobey this command, then her willingness to submit to Christ in everything is called into question just as it would be by any continual and deliberate disregard of God's word—indeed, as it would be for a husband who refused to love his wife! Moreover, if a wife's submission is to reflect her submission to the Lord, she will submit herself to her husband voluntarily, willingly, deliberately, joyfully, wholeheartedly, thoughtfully and with wisdom and discernment.

The second parameter is that a wife is to submit "in everything" (v. 24). She is not to mark out 'no-go' zones with her husband. Just as there is no limit and no 'no-go' zones in the church's submission to Christ, so a wife's submission to her husband is to be "in everything". What submission requires is an attitude of trust, respect and honour that graciously recognizes the husband's God-given authority, and willingly accepts his leadership and responsibility.

If you're a wife then at this point there might be a little voice inside your head crying out, "That's all very well, but you don't know my husband!" You would be right, of course—I don't! And if you're a husband, the weight of this responsibility might well overwhelm you! You know even better than your wife just how far short of perfect you fall, and yet she is meant to look to you to lead your family.

Paul knew that no husband is perfect and God (whose word this is) knows it even more. Even so, you will notice that the submission required of a wife is not conditional on her husband getting it right.

The passage does not say, "Wives, submit to your own husbands when they love you or when you think they deserve it". It does not say, "When *they* do their bit, then and only then *you* do yours". The only fine print in this command to submit is "as to the Lord" and "in everything".

Having said that, however, there are two qualifications that need to be made. The first is that because a wife's submission is "as to the Lord", then if a husband's demands are in conflict with obedience to Christ, Christ wins every time. If a husband wants his wife to join him in sinning, she is not to follow him into sin. If he wants her to be sexually immoral, to cheat on her tax, to lie or steal, or to neglect or abuse her children, then her first duty always is to obey Christ and his righteousness. If a husband wants his wife to forsake Christ, in part or completely, she is to submit to her eternal groom not her earthly one.

The second qualification is that tragically some husbands exercise their 'headship' as crushing and destructive abuse, which can be expressed in any number of ways: physically, sexually, verbally, socially, financially, and even spiritually.[2] This is the sort of tyrannical rule that Christ rejected and came to overthrow. We would be naïve to think this sort of abuse does not happen even in Christian families, and even with people we know—and think

---

2   It would be wrong to assume that only men are guilty of mistreating their wives and/or children this way. There are women who abuse their husbands and/or children. Their gender does not make their abuse any less sinful. Sadly, because of the impact of feminism and gender stereotypes, our society is less receptive to the plight of abused men so these men often find it more difficult to get the help they need.

we know *well*. It is *never* right. It is *not biblical* headship. It is abuse.

If this is your experience or the experience of someone you know (female or male), do not, *for Christ's sake*, let it continue unaddressed. It must stop. I appreciate that it will take great courage to seek help, but help must be sought. Speak to your pastor. Speak to a wise Christian friend. Get professional and pastoral help for yourself or for your friend. To leave the situation unaddressed is **not** submission. Instead it is allowing sin to continue unchecked, and in that way does no-one any good—not the children or the wife or the husband.

Such treatment denies the equality and value of the abused person in the eyes of God, and their value as equal partners in the marriage relationship (albeit with different responsibilities). One of the surprising things in the New Testament, given its first-century origins, is that wives are treated as equals in this passage and in the others that deal with marriage (Col 3:18-19; 1 Pet 3:1-7). As we noted earlier, Paul charges wives as moral agents and considers them equally members of Christ (Eph 5:30; cf. Col 3:18). Elsewhere, too, wives have equal 'rights' to their husbands in regards to sexual relations (Mark 10:11-12; 1 Cor 7:2-5). Nowhere are women regarded as chattels that can be treated or disposed of as a man sees fit.

As we saw in 1 Corinthians 11, woman and man are equally made in the image of God, and both come from God (1 Cor 11:7, 12). They are equal in his sight: equally fallen, equally in need of redemption, and equally accepted into his family (Gal 3:25-29).

Possible objections

Now before we explore more closely how this pattern of marriage can be worked out in our modern situations, we need to consider some of the arguments used to overrule or reject this teaching. There are five main objections.

The first concerns the meaning of the Greek word for 'head' (*kephalē*) in Ephesians 5:23. This is essentially the same argument we encountered with this word in 1 Corinthians 11:3. The claim is that the word 'head' does not mean 'authority', and should be translated 'source' or 'origin' in the sense that the head of a river is the source of that river.

As we saw when we considered this earlier, studies looking at the use of this word in ancient literature make it clear that when the word is not being used for a physical head, it usually has the meaning of 'authority over'. And even in those places where it may have the sense of 'origin' or 'nourishment', the notion of authority is not absent.

What's more, in Ephesians 5, where the headship of Christ and the husband is the premise for the response of submission from the church and the wife respectively, it is special pleading to say that authority is not on view.

The second common objection concerns Paul's command to submit "to one another out of reverence for Christ" (v. 21). This view claims that the real meaning of these instructions to husbands and wives is one of mutual submission where the wife is to submit to the husband and the husband is to submit to the wife.

But there are several problems with this 'mutual submission' idea, not least of which is that the plain meaning of the subsequent verses goes against it: Christ does not submit to the church, neither are parents to submit to their children or masters to their slaves (cf. Eph 6:1-7; Col 3:18-22). These are non-reversible ordered relationships, as is the marriage relationship. Certainly, selfless love is a common mark of being filled by the Spirit (cf. Eph 4:2-3), but it exists alongside of (not to the exclusion of) responsibilities of submission and authority in specific relationships. Besides, nowhere are husbands told to submit to their wives, and submission language (*hupotassō/hupotagē*) is uniformly used in the New Testament for asymmetrical relationships.

So 5:21 is not promoting the idea of mutual submission.

Rather, it functions as a heading or summary that introduces the idea of submission, and the following verses then explain how this submission is to be worked out in three pairs of household relationships.

The third objection is that these instructions were fine in their original cultural setting but for various reasons they no longer apply. But as we have seen in the reasons Paul gives for these instructions, God intends this teaching to transcend culture.

Another popular objection should be familiar by now: it is based on Galatians 3:28. It claims there is a conflict between the statement "There is neither Jew nor Greek, there is neither slave nor free, there is no male and female" and texts that teach gender differences in the church and the family, and that this conflict can only be resolved by giving primacy to one lot of texts. It is a choice between gender 'equality' and (alleged) 'inequality'.

But there are at least two problems with this argument. First, this is not the way to read the Bible. If the Bible is God's infallible word then when we encounter two things that seem to contradict each other, we need to work out how they fit together rather than picking the one we like and jettisoning the other. Second, as we have seen, Galatians 3:25-29 is about the end of religious and social categories that kept people apart, and privileged some and not others. In Christ, there is no longer male and female, slave nor free, Jew nor Greek because we are all *one* in Christ Jesus. You see, unlike Ephesians 5, Galatians 3 is not about the *relationships* of men and women; it is about the *unity* we all enjoy in our relationship with Christ Jesus.

The final objection we all might be tempted to make is one of selective hearing, where we say, "I'm happy to obey the Bible in most things, but this is a bridge too far. God doesn't understand my marriage so I'll obey those bits I can, and just put this in the too hard basket." But we just can't do that. What is not obvious in our translations (with their verse numbers, paragraphs, headings and so on) is that wifely submission actually flows out of the command Paul gave several verses back: "be filled with the Spirit" (v. 18).

So the flow of the passage is: be careful how you live, do not be foolish, do not get drunk *but* be filled with the Spirit (vv. 15-18). Now we tend to think that being filled with the Spirit means all sorts of spectacular spiritual experiences like prophecy, tongues, healings and so on. But not here. Paul immediately explains what being filled with the Spirit means: it means "*addressing* one another in psalms and hymns and spiritual songs, *singing* and *making melody* to the Lord with your heart, *giving thanks* always and for everything to God the Father, and *submitting* to one another out of reverence for Christ" (vv. 19-21).

That is, being filled by the Spirit *changes* relationships. The Spirit enables us to encourage other Christians and to praise God (that's no surprise). But the Spirit also (and this *is* a surprise) enables us to accept authority and willingly submit to it—if we are wives, to our husbands; if we are children, to our parents; and if we are employees, to our bosses.

Now I assume that as Christians we all want to be filled with the Spirit. We don't want to be foolish. We want to be wise and careful, and live as children of light (v. 8). Well, this is what it will look like: it will change the way we speak to our fellow believers, it will change the way we relate to God, and it will fashion our relationships with others and enable us to accept the authority of those whom God in his wisdom has put over us.

More than a feeling

Of course, none of this is easy to put into practice. The submission required of wives is at odds with our culture, and more importantly it is at odds with our sinful human nature. Likewise, the loving headship on view is at odds with our culture, and with fallen human nature. So there is no couple for which this will not require effort and change.

Ever since the Fall of Genesis 3 a wife's desire has been to control her husband, and each wife has her own signature way of doing that. Perhaps she nags or manipulates. Perhaps she puts him down in front of his friends or the kids. Perhaps she never says a word but keeps a catalogue of his sins that stokes a growing fire of anger and self-righteousness.

And ever since the Fall husbands have been abusing their authority, either by being harsh and self-centred, or by selfishly disengaging and abdicating authority—leaving a void to be filled by his wife or children. These days, too, husbands are often emotionally and physically absent from the home, with the desire to provide financially and build a career overshadowing the desire to provide real leadership on the ground.

So in our evangelical culture, many of us have settled for marriages that believe in headship and submission *in principle* but have nothing like it *in practice*. We have reduced headship and submission to attitudes that have no tangible expression. We give lip-service to the biblical model but our patterns of relating are so ingrained, and so influenced by our secular authority-hating culture, and the pressures of marriage and family life are so great, that it is all just too hard—especially when our marriage is stable and we dare not rock the boat!

But this is no way to treat God's demand of us. He demands radical obedience. And while submission and loving headship might begin as attitudes, they are attitudes that *are to be expressed.* Our marriages should be *changed* because of them. And as if we needed more incentive than obedience to live this way, our marriages should be *better* if we do, because that is how God designed marriage to work at its best.

Imagine where we would be if the Lord Jesus only ever had an *attitude* of loving headship towards the church but was never moved to *do* anything about it!

6 | WON WITHOUT A WORD: 1 PETER 3

O NE OF THE BLESSINGS of knowing our biological parents—a blessing I recognize is not shared by all—is that we can spot family likenesses. For example, I have my paternal grandmother's blue eyes, small features, small hands and small feet. I may wish that I also inherited her lovely thick wavy hair, but the fact is that I look more like her than I do any other relative. I can still remember at her sister's funeral what a strange experience it was to find myself in a room with a generation of elderly women (her cousins) who all had the same blue eyes and small features.

There was no doubt that I belonged!

Family resemblance, whether in appearance, abilities or traits, is a powerful part of belonging. It demonstrates to others that we belong in the family, and it builds in us a strong bond with those who share the same family markers. In fact, my observation is that family resemblances have the effect of establishing and declaring our identity—both externally and internally, publicly and personally.

It's the same with God's family. There are family markers, family resemblances. But what are they?

Of course, there are things like the beards and flannelette shirts that young Christian men uniformly wore a few decades back. There are t-shirts with ministry logos. Gold and silver crosses dangling off ears and necklaces. WWJD bracelets. Fish stickers on cars…

But these are all a bit superficial and cheesy—not to mention culturally limited and easily out of date! There must be more to mark us out as God's family than these.

Well, of course there is—but who would have thought that the shape of our marriages was part of it? Who would have thought that, as we take all the good and bad habits and hang ups of our families of origin into our marriages (whether consciously or not), what we should be striving to display in our marriages is our *spiritual* heritage and family resemblance?

But that's what we find in 1 Peter.

Peter, Paul and Sarah

This is the second text we are going to examine that addresses the relationship, roles and responsibilities of wives and husbands. The first was by the apostle Paul. This one is by the apostle Peter.

In many ways this text sounds a lot like Ephesians 5, which, as we saw in the previous chapter, is a favourite at Christian weddings and deals with the relationship of husband and wife and the similarities of that relationship to the relationship of Christ and the church.

The Ephesians text is one of several Paul wrote that set out the responsibilities of believers within various household relationships. The other passages are Colossians 3:18-4:1, Titus 2 and possibly sections of 1 Timothy 5-6.

Now if these passages by Paul were all that we had, we might be tempted to think (as some do) that Paul had a problem with women and that his teaching about women tells us more about his psychology and prejudices than about God's will for our lives.

But even leaving 1 Peter 3 aside, the claim that Paul was a misogynist is simply not supported by the evidence even though it is often stated as fact.

Some years ago, I presented a paper about some of Paul's letters in a university post-graduate seminar. It was my first foray into the academic world beyond the evangelical theological college I had attended. Immediately after I read the paper, a fellow student dismissed all I had said, saying that Paul had an inflated view of his own importance, that he was a self-appointed misogynist who had no authority even in the first century, and that his letters hold no interest for us now beyond telling us how he single-handedly hijacked Jesus' message of equality and love. Paul's letters tell us about his misogynistic ego trip, not about the Christian faith.

But such a view will not do, not only because it denies the divine inspiration, authority and infallibility of Scripture, but also because the evidence shows it is wrong. The New Testament repeatedly records Paul's respect and love for his sisters in Christ, and his recognition of their valued contribution to the advance of the gospel (cf. Acts 18:1-3, 18; Rom 16:1-7, 12-13, 15; 1 Cor 1:11; Phil 4:2-3; Col 4:15; 2 Tim 1:5, 3:14-15, 4:19-20; Phlm 2). Far from hating women, it is clear that Paul *loved* women! And that's even before we factor in his repeated exhortations to his Christian brothers *and sisters*,[1] his acceptance of women praying and prophesying, and the rich inclusiveness of texts like Galatians 3:25-29.

Paul's high regard for women, however, did not overrule God-ordained differences between women and men. The one sat comfortably alongside the other. Gender equality in God's family and non-identical gender roles and responsibilities were not

---

1   As I have previously noted, the ESV regrettably translates the vocative address *adelphoi* as "brothers" rather than "brothers and sisters", which is relegated to footnotes (e.g. Col 1:2, 4:15; 1 Thess 1:4; 2:1, 9, 14, 17; 3:7; 4:1, [6], 10, 13; 5:1, 4, 12, 14, 25, 26, 27; 1 Tim 4:6).

opposing trump cards, because these roles and responsibilities did not give greater or lesser value or dignity to either gender.

And this is where 1 Peter 3 really adds to our understanding of this important biblical teaching.

First, 1 Peter 3:1-7 is less well known than the Ephesians 5 passage and so it has the advantage of unfamiliarity. We are less likely to zone out and think we know what it says, and so more likely to hear what it is saying.

Second, it is not written by Paul, so it gives us confidence (if we needed it) that Paul was right. Indeed, it is a second apostolic witness telling us that God wants wives and husbands to have different roles and responsibilities in marriage.

Third, while we might have thought from Paul's letters that this pattern of relationships only applies in Christian marriages, 1 Peter 3 tells us this is not the case. 1 Peter 3 joins 1 Corinthians 7 as God's special provision for mixed-faith marriages. It clearly addresses the situation where the husband is an unbeliever and the wife is a Christian, which is not an uncommon situation in our churches. Of course, it is not just mixed-faith marriages that are on view, because Peter also has instructions for believing husbands of believing wives (v. 7).

Fourth, if we had been able to come away from Ephesians 5 thinking all that is required are *attitudes* of submissiveness and loving headship—that they are about a mindset and not about actions—then the focus on actions and appearances in 1 Peter 3 shuts off that escape hatch.

Fifth, 1 Peter 3 introduces our matriarch Sarah to the discussion of gender roles, and in doing so identifies an aspect of a wife's submission we might have (conveniently) overlooked in Ephesians—namely, obedience.

So now let us turn to the text itself.

At first glance

¹Likewise, wives, be subject to your own husbands, so
that even if some do not obey the word, they may be won
without a word by the conduct of their wives, ²when they
see your respectful and pure conduct. ³Do not let your
adorning be external—the braiding of hair and the putting
on of gold jewellery, or the clothing you wear—⁴but let
your adorning be the hidden person of the heart with the
imperishable beauty of a gentle and quiet spirit, which in
God's sight is very precious. ⁵For this is how the holy women
who hoped in God used to adorn themselves, by submitting
to their own husbands, ⁶as Sarah obeyed Abraham, calling
him lord. And you are her children, if you do good and do
not fear anything that is frightening.

⁷Likewise, husbands, live with your wives in an
understanding way, showing honour to the woman as the
weaker vessel, since they are heirs with you of the grace of
life, so that your prayers may not be hindered. (1 PET 3:1-7)

We can see immediately some real differences between this
passage and Ephesians 5. Here, it is the wives who are in the frame
and given more details about their conduct than the husbands.
What's more, there is a focus on a wife's beauty. There is mention
of Sarah and Abraham. For the first time in all the passages we have
looked at so far, there is not even an oblique reference to Genesis
1-3. Also there is no mention of male 'headship', no model of
Christ and the church, and husbands are told to understand and
honour their wives, rather than love them sacrificially.

But of course there are similarities as well.

As with Ephesians, the familiar question of whether women
and men generally or wives and husbands specifically are on view
is settled for us, both by the context of the text—which deals

with other household relationships—and by the fact that wives are instructed about their response to *their own* husbands, and husbands are told how to relate to the particular woman with whom they live—their wives.

Peter, like Paul, also speaks to the wives first and charges them to submit themselves willingly, consciously and voluntarily to their husbands. Then, like Paul, he speaks to the husbands and gives them different instructions from those he gave the wives. So for Peter, as for Paul, there is one response required of wives and another response of husbands. These instructions are not unisex. They are not identical. Rather, they are *complementary*.

Note too that neither Peter nor Paul holds the husbands accountable for their wives' submission or tells husbands to make their wives submit. Submission within marriage for both Peter and Paul is a response of a wife to her husband, and it originates entirely from the wife.

A closer look at submission

As we have already seen in earlier chapters, 'submission' these days is a dirty word—for men often as much as for women, and for Christians as much as non-Christians.

Even those of us who are not affected by feminist-fuelled power struggles, who *do not* think submission is a dirty word, and who *do* think it should shape our marriages, are not quite sure what it looks like. So even though we want to, we struggle to put it into practice.

In reality, many wives *talk* about being submissive more than they *are* submissive—in the same way that politicians might talk up their policy commitments without ever delivering on them. It's a case of: "If I talk about it loud and long enough, I might just persuade people (myself included) that I'm actually doing it".

Moreover, in conservative evangelical circles, the idea of submission can have a frosted-lens romance to it that has more in common with rescued fairytale princesses in the arms of their one true love (as the music swells) than with God's ideal of marriage, or the day-to-day grind of marriage between two sinners. But this will not do! This side of glory, godly submission will *never* come easily. (Neither will a husband's godly, loving leadership!)

So, given we have so much cultural baggage about this word 'submission', which we've picked up from secular *and* Christian sources, we have to make sure we understand it the way Peter meant it to be understood.

We cannot hear the word and have our default setting determine our reaction. Our hearing and reaction must be shaped by what we know about submission *from God's word*.

1. "Likewise"

Our first clue about the nature of wifely submission comes from the way that Peter introduces his instructions, when he tells wives "likewise" (or "in the same way", NIV), "be subject to your own husbands" (v. 1). At first glance, it looks as though we only have to look at the verses immediately before—perhaps the instructions to slaves or the description of Christ in chapter 2—to work out what a wife's submission looks like. But that is actually misleading.

First, there is a translation question to answer. The word translated "likewise" (*homoios*) has more than one meaning. It can mean 'in the same way' or 'similarly' when a comparison or inference is being drawn, or it can simply mean 'also'. It is a joining word, but the context has to decide what sort of join it is.

In the original language this word is used twice in this passage (vv. 1, 7), so it makes sense to translate it the same way both times. When we do that, we find that "likewise" or "in the same way" does not fit because the instructions for husbands are so different from those for the wives.

So rather than "likewise" or "in the same way" the best translation of this joining word is "also". In which case, the advice to wives says:

"Also, wives, be subject to your own husbands"; and the advice to husbands says: "Also, husbands, live with your wives…"

So although we might have thought a wife's submission is to be in the same manner that someone or something else submits, that is not the case. Peter is not saying that Christian wives are like slaves who have to submit to their husbands in the same way that Christian slaves submit to their masters. Neither are Christian wives to submit in the same way as Christ, because you will notice that his example serves as a model of perseverance in the face of unjust suffering, rather than of submission to authority (2:21-25).

Wives are not to submit in the same way as anything, but *they are to submit*. So how does the context help us understand what that looks like?

2. "For the Lord's sake"

Although the headings in our Bibles obscure it, the beginning of this passage is way back in the middle of the previous chapter when Peter says, "Be subject for the Lord's sake to every human institution" (2:13). This is the first mention of submission and it functions like a heading or summary statement for the following instructions, which deal with the Christian and the state, slaves with masters, wives and husbands.

Imagine what it would have been like for the first Christians. They must have wondered if God really wanted them to submit to pagan human authorities that were cruel and corrupt.

Should a Christian recognize the authority of the emperor when the emperor does not recognize the authority of God? Does a non-Christian governor have the right to punish wrongdoers when the governor himself is an unrepentant sinner? Does a Christian wife have to respect and submit to a husband who himself does not respect and accept the lordship of Christ?

These are logical and understandable questions.

Peter's answer is that all human beings (believers or unbelievers) are creatures of God whom he has placed in various relationships of authority. So when the relationship requires it, submission is still the right response for Christians. It can and should be done "for the Lord's sake"—that is, as an expression of faithful godly Christian living.

So in terms of our passage, Christians *generally* are to submit in ordered relationships in society for the Lord's sake (even to unbelieving emperors and governors), Christian slaves are to submit to their (unjust) masters before God, 'and also' Christian wives are to submit to their husbands—*even if* their husbands are unbelievers.

But it's not just women married to unbelievers that Peter has in mind. By the time we get to the wife's beauty and the example of Sarah and the godly women of the past, it is obvious that Peter has all wives in mind. After all, Sarah was married to Abraham, and you could hardly call him an unbeliever!

So in Peter's mind there is not one rule for Christian marriages and another for mixed-faith marriages. In marriages of both kinds, wives are to submit to their husbands.

A closer look at wives

So what does a wife's submission look like?

Well, at first glance there is not a lot to go on. Clearly, it has something to do with behaviour and demeanour. Also, the example of the godly wives of the past (and Sarah in particular) tells us that it has something to do with obedience, respect and doing right. But as for the day-to-day nuts and bolts of submission, Peter—like Paul in the passages we have already looked at—gives us very little of the detail.

He does however give us some idea of what submission is not.[2]

---

2   The structure for the following section has been adapted from Wayne Grudem's article 'Wives like Sarah, and the Husbands Who Honor Them: 1 Peter 3:1-7', in J Piper and WA Grudem (eds), *Recovering Biblical Manhood and Womanhood: A Response to Evangelical Feminism*, Crossway, Wheaton, 1991, pp. 194-208.

Submission does not mean a wife is to love her husband more than Christ. Whether or not her husband is a believer, Peter is not saying the Christian wife is to love and submit to her husband in preference to her love of and submission to Christ. As the old hymn puts it, it is "Thou and thou only first in my heart"—where the 'thou' is always Christ.[3]

All Christian submission is for "the Lord's sake" (2:13), so it is an expression of our love, obedience and faithfulness *to the Lord Jesus.* Sure, we are to submit to earthly authorities but God's will is to be our guide (2:15). We are first and foremost servants of the living God, pleasing and obeying him before we submit to any other authority, and all our relationships are to be governed by our fear of God (2:16-17).

The deciding factor in all Christian submission is obedience to God, whether or not there is a conflict of demands. As we saw in the previous chapter, this means there may be times when submitting to Christ prevents a wife submitting to her husband. There may be times when a wife must say "No" because saying "Yes" would mean she or her husband would be disobedient to Christ. Which leads to my next point.

Submission does not mean that wives are to turn their brains off. Peter expects these women to think about how they live. This is not a picture of the little woman who has stopped thinking and acting for herself, and who when her husband tells her to jump only asks, "How high?"

On the contrary, Peter addresses the wives directly because he expects them to reflect, understand and act on what he is saying to them. Their submission is an intelligent, willing, voluntary response. It is their responsibility—no-one else's—and they must choose for themselves what it means for them. Peter expects

---

3   'Be Thou My Vision', English words by Eleanor Hull, 1912.

the women to think, and to think *wisely*.

The very fact that Peter addresses wives of unbelieving husbands means he knows that some of the women have understood the truth when their husbands have not. The significance of this might be lost on us as we are used to women doing and acting as they please. But in the first century and in some cultures today, such independence of thought by women was and is both counter-cultural and a personally courageous and difficult thing to do.

Wives are to submit themselves to their husbands; they are not to stop thinking, learning, reading or reasoning. Neither can they abdicate responsibility for their spiritual growth and wellbeing to their husbands.

Submission does not mean that a wife cannot influence her husband. I think sometimes submission can be seen as a one-way street, where the husband is able to influence the woman's life but the wife has no influence over the man. But Peter makes it clear that this is not the case.

He is enlisting these women in the greatest task of all: winning souls for Christ. Not only are wives to be intelligent and thoughtful in their submission, they are also to submit to their husbands in the hope of influencing them "*so that* even if some do not obey the word, they may be won without a word by the conduct of their wives" (3:1).

It might be more difficult to see in some Bible versions, but Peter is using a play on words based on the word 'word' to make his point. You see, he wants those who are disobedient to *the* Word to be won over *without a* word.

His point is not that wives shouldn't talk to their husbands, but that those husbands who are hardened to the gospel, impervious to *the* Word, might be won over *without* a word—that is, instead by *conduct*. It is as though he is saying to the wives, "When all is said and done, keep living faithfully and let your actions do the talking"; a case of letting your actions speak louder than words.

Peter wants these submitting women to influence their husbands, either by talk or by behaviour. We find the same idea earlier where all Christians are to keep their conduct honourable so that non-Christians will see their good deeds and glorify God (2:12). In both instances, Peter assumes that a quiet Christian life filled with good works and lived for God actually speaks volumes to those who do not know God, and (get this!) that such obedient Christian living is attractive to unbelievers and can persuade them to believe the gospel!

So, one way or the other, Peter wants these wives to persuade their husbands into the kingdom—and paradoxically their submission is part of this persuasion. What may also surprise us is that Peter sees the woman's beauty as a means of this persuasion.

Now being persuaded by beauty is not always a good thing.

I take it that the beauty of Salome dancing before Herod is what caused Herod to make promises he never should have made, which led to the beheading of John the Baptist (Mark 6:22; Matt 14:6-8).[4] And of course, it was the beauty of the fruit in the garden of Eden and the promise it offered that proved too much temptation for Eve and Adam (Gen 3:6).

What is the difference between beauty worth being persuaded by and beauty that is not? The difference is the *kind* of beauty involved. The beauty of Salome and of the fruit in the garden was plain to see, but succumbing to it led to death. But fortunately, and in God's providence, it is not physical beauty that is meant to be persuasive. If physical beauty was meant to persuade people into the kingdom, our powers of persuasion would start diminishing from about the time we turned 15!

But the beauty Peter has in mind is what is *beautiful to God*. We all

---

4   Josephus, *Antiquities*, 18.136f.

know that beauty is in the eye of the beholder. Here, the beholder is God. God is the one who determines what real beauty is, not the mirror or the fashion magazines (praise God!).

The thing with all the 'makeover' programs on TV—whether they involve scalpels and silicone, Botox and collagen, or just new wardrobes and hairdos—is that they only renovate the shopfront. They make the outside look beautiful but do nothing to change the heart. But God is interested in making us *new* so he is not interested in shopfronts, which can only be improved with outward adornment like hairstyles, jewellery and clothes; things that you put on the outside.

Earlier in his letter, Peter states the obvious when he says, "All flesh is like grass and all its glory like the flower of grass. The grass withers, and the flower falls, but the word of the Lord remains forever" (1 Pet 1:24-25). God is interested in what lasts, not what is passing away. And so the beauty God is looking for is inner beauty—beauty that is imperishable and unfading, like the inheritance God gives us that will never perish, spoil or fade (1:4).

And the interesting thing is that while the world looks for beauty in things you stick on the outside (clothes, jewellery, makeup, hair—even a trim figure), what God looks at is "the hidden person of the heart" (3:4). In our culture, that's the person most often forgotten.

But God tells us here that true beauty is a heart that is pure, reverent, respectful, quiet and humble. And while these qualities might not look impressively expensive from a human standpoint, in God's sight they are rich, extravagant, lavish and precious.

Recently a friend of mine was given a diamond ring by her husband. I am no expert on diamond rings—I just thought it was a nice ring with a pretty big diamond. But when my friend showed it to me, just so I didn't miss the value of the gift, she told me how many carats the diamond was. As it happens, I do not know anything about carats so this extra information meant nothing to me. But even I picked up her point that "This ring is really worth something!" But the apostle Peter would disagree. His point is that moral purity, reverent fear, a quiet spirit, and gentle humility are *really worth something*—they are head-turning expensive adornments as far as God is concerned. They are the 'must-haves' of a truly beautiful woman.

God tells us true beauty is beauty of the heart that is expressed in godly conduct, and it is so exquisite and striking that even an unbelieving husband can see it.

Family resemblance

I guess women like this were in short supply in Peter's day no less than ours. There weren't too many role models around. So in the same way he gives Christian servants the example of Christ in chapter 2, Peter gives his readers some examples of what he is asking of wives.

First he points to the holy women of the past who put their trust in God, and made themselves beautiful not with trinkets and trappings of external beauty but with inner beauty that comes from trusting in God and willingly submitting to their husbands. Then he points to Sarah as the example *par excellence* of that submission because she obeyed Abraham and called him 'lord'. But when did Sarah do this?

Some people think that Peter is referring to the episode in Genesis 18:12, when Sarah called Abraham 'lord' or 'master'. But this is a one-off incident, and it has little to do with Sarah *obeying* Abraham. So it is unlikely that Peter expects Christian wives to build their entire marriages on this one incident.

It is much more likely that Peter is referring to an ongoing attitude that enabled Sarah to leave her kinsfolk and homeland and follow Abraham without fear into dangerous and uncertain situations, trusting that God would care for her. Abraham adopted the life of faith and bid Sarah follow him, and she did.

Now some interpretations try to make this part of 1 Peter 3 say anything other than what it plainly says. They claim that Abraham obeyed Sarah as often as she obeyed him, or that Sarah did not obey Abraham and so Peter is having a little joke with his readers. Or they suggest that Peter is making a contrast between what was demanded of wives under the old covenant and now that Christ has come.

But to be honest, it is hard to take these arguments too seriously.

A closer look at the few times Abraham is meant to have obeyed Sarah shows why. On the first occasion, Abraham "listened to the voice" of his wife and slept with her servant Hagar, rather than waiting for God to fulfil his promises through Sarah's barren womb (Gen 16:2). In effect, he *obeyed* his wife only to be led straight into *disobedience* to God. You will remember that Adam also "listened to the voice" of his wife with disastrous consequences (3:17), so this is hardly a ringing endorsement of the practice!

And a closer look at the second time Abraham is meant to have obeyed Sarah shows that the person Abraham obeys is actually God, not Sarah at all (21:10-12). It just so happens that God's purposes will be achieved by Abraham doing what Sarah asked of him—even though she asked for the wrong reasons—because by casting out Hagar and her son, Ishmael, Abraham's family line will be carried through Isaac alone.

Also, it is nonsense to say that Peter is making a contrast between his readers and the godly women in the past. He encourages Christian wives to be *like* Sarah. That is why he wants them to realize they are Sarah's daughters. And he wants Christian wives to be submissive to their husbands, because that is how the godly women of the past also lived. These faithful women made themselves beautiful by paying attention to the heart not the mirror, and their inner beauty could be seen in their submission to their husbands. And part of that submission was obedience, as we see in Sarah's example—obedience in keeping with God's good purposes, as befits holy women who trust in God.

Sarah and the holy women of the past were examples for first-century Christian wives, and they are for 'modern' 21st-century wives, too.

But they are more than just examples; they are also *reasons* to live like this. These women are giants of the faith, and wives who want to belong to the same holy nation as them, the same chosen people, are to live like them. Let me show you what I mean.

My mother has been tracing our family tree. She has boxes of photos, letters, poems, medals and so on. The more she gets into it, the more she finds various abilities and personality traits in herself or in us that come from her ancestors. You get the sense that this family paraphernalia is giving her reason and licence to be the sort of people her ancestors were, to live as they lived. If she lives like them, she shows she belongs with them.

In the same way, Sarah and the holy women of the past are role models for Christian wives to follow, but they are a reason to live like this as well. Their lives were lives of faith and if we want to belong to the people of faith, then our lives are to be like theirs.

Although Peter does not mention Genesis 2, when we look there (as we will in the next chapter) we find that in marriage God intended the woman and the man to have different complementary responsibilities: submission for the wife, and leadership for the man. God's good creation was not good while the man was alone. He needed a helper. And so God formed the woman as a helper suitable for the man: equal to him, bone of his bone, flesh of his flesh, made together with him in the image of God as a companion to work with him in ruling and subduing the creation; equal in every way, but with the distinct and different responsibility of helping.

Obviously none of us live in the garden of Eden. We live on the other side of the Fall with all the distortions that human disobedience brought to God's good creation. But as Peter's instructions to wives make clear, God's original design for marriage is still the ideal. It was good for Adam and Eve. It was good for the holy women of the past. And it is good for us. Wifely submission is still the mark of godly living, even in mixed-faith marriages.

And when Christian women submit to their husbands, they make themselves truly beautiful—at the very least, in God's sight—and this beauty is the family likeness or resemblance of faithful women in God's family.

Considering husbands

But of course, it takes two to tango—or to be married—and so Peter turns to address Christian husbands.

Straight away we can see that the section dealing with husbands is much shorter than that addressing wives, and also that Peter assumes all Christian husbands will have believing wives. He does this because in first-century culture the religion of the husband usually determined the religion of the rest of the family—which is part of what makes the advice to believing wives with *unbelieving* husbands so counter-cultural!

Peter has two instructions for the husbands. They are to:

(i) live considerately with their wives
(ii) give honour to their wives.

It is worth noting that this is not 'mutual submission' as some modern egalitarian interpretations claim. It does not say, "Wives, be subject to your own husbands, and husbands, be subject to your own wives". Not only does Peter give *different* instructions to wives and to husbands, but to get the word 'submission' to mean 'live considerately' and 'give honour' you have to stretch the meaning of the word to such an extent that it ceases to mean what it means. Both inside and outside the Bible, submission is not identically reciprocal, requiring the same response from one to the other. Rather, it involves the acceptance by one party of the authority and responsibility of another.

So, whereas wives are to submit to their husbands, husbands are to show their wives understanding and honour in the way they live with them.

And why does Peter say this is so? He gives us two reasons, the first of which needs a little unpacking, and the second of which hopefully will pose no problem for us. Let's take the easy (second) reason first.

Husbands are to show their wives understanding and honour because they are joint heirs in God's gracious gift of life. The truth that husbands and wives are *joint* heirs might not strike us as particularly radical—indeed, it is just what we would expect from God's word, where both men and women are made in the image of God and equally redeemed by his Son. But in the ancient world, wives were considered intellectually and even morally inferior, and so their submission to their husbands took place not in the context of their equality but in the context of their *in*equality.

Not so in Christian marriage. There is a fundamental equality between husbands and wives. They are equally heirs in God's kingdom—which is the wonderful truth that Paul affirms in Galatians 3:25-29.

This means that the ordered relationships in marriage are not based on merit or status. They are based on God's good design for his equally loved and equally adopted children.

The first and more obscure reason (at least for us) Peter gives for his instructions to husbands in 1 Peter 3 is that the female is "the weaker vessel" (v. 7). Perhaps it is stating the obvious to say that many people today have difficulties with this expression, not just because we are not sure what it means but also because we don't like what we think it means!

Some claim that Peter means women are morally or intellectually inferior to men and that is why they are to submit in marriage. But this means reading something into the text that is not there and which the text actually disallows, since Peter's instruction to wives implies their moral virtue and intelligent choice!

Another view says that Peter is talking about physical weakness, telling husbands to protect their wives because women are generally physically weaker than men. This is perhaps what is on view, but there is another possibility.

I think it is more likely Peter is recognizing the fact that in any ordered relationship of authority and submission, the one who submits has a weaker or lesser authority. The act of submission leaves them vulnerable to the quality of leadership that the other provides.

It is interesting that in the previous two sets of relationships, Peter does not give instructions to the ones exercising authority— either to the emperor and governors or to the servants' masters (2:13-20). Perhaps he does not expect his letter to be read by people in those positions. But he knows there are Christian husbands, and so he balances his call for wifely submission with counter-cultural instructions to husbands about their responsibilities. As the ones called upon to submit, wives are vulnerable to the way their husbands lead, so Peter says to every Christian husband, "Don't abuse the authority and trust you have been given, look after your wife, understand her vulnerable situation, and treat her with respect and honour in all aspects of your life together". This is not the same as submitting to her, in the sense of giving a wife authority over her husband. But it does require the man to submit his will to that of Christ, and to care for and lead his wife with understanding and dignity.

The assumptions behind these instructions then, as with the instructions to wives, are the equality of the husband and wife before the ultimate authority of God, and the God-given authority of a husband within the marriage relationship.

But please note, Peter does not stress the husband's authority. He does not say to husbands (as some husbands wrongly understand it) "These are your rights, so go for it". On the contrary! Peter warns husbands that if they use their authority for their own benefit rather than for the benefit of their wives, their own prayers will be hindered. Their relationship with God will suffer. After all, "God opposes the proud but gives grace to the humble" (5:5). It seems reasonable to assume the converse is also true: if husbands relate with loving understanding and respect for their wives, then both their home life and their spiritual life will flourish.

Possible objections

Many of the standard objections to the complementary pattern of gender relationships that we find in 1 Peter 3 will be familiar by now. There is the suggestion that *mutual* submission and not just *wifely* submission is on view. There is the suggestion that Galatians 3:28 overrules the gender differences we see in this text. There is the charge of inconsistency since women today braid their hair and wear gold jewellery. We have already answered these objections either in this chapter or in earlier ones.

But there are two remaining objections that need to be answered.

1. Just like slavery

Perhaps the most common objection to applying this passage today is to say that the idea of women submitting to men is like slavery. The argument goes like this: in the New Testament, slavery is not condemned—in fact, slaves are told to submit to their masters. But today we all recognize that slavery is wrong, and we have no problem disregarding those parts of the New Testament about slaves and masters. It's the same with men and women. The pattern of gender relationships in the New Testament was okay in the first century, but it was just a cultural practice—a *bad* cultural practice—that must be rejected, as we have rejected slavery.

On this view, the only reason Peter (or Paul) urges wives to submit is because to do otherwise would have been too culturally shocking, and would have distracted from the truly radical message of the gospel, which is that Jesus Christ is Lord.

But this is wrong for several reasons.

It is clear that Peter wants Christians to do anything but fit into their culture. It is not overstating things to say that Christians were to be *so different* from their surrounding culture that they stood out (2:11-12, 4:1-4). In light of this, it would be extraordinary if Peter (or Paul) tolerated and taught things that were contrary to the gospel and to God's purposes for his people just to avoid rocking cultural boats.

Moreover, there are serious consequences of this view for our understanding of Scripture as God's perfect expired and inspired word. If certain instructions in the Bible are actually *contrary* to God's will, how then do we decide what is true and what is not? Or if these are not God's commands but the apostles taking matters into their own hands, where else might this be the case? Can God not ensure that his word speaks his truth clearly and accurately?

Of course he can—and we can have confidence in the truthfulness and goodness of all of God's written word. We do not need special red print to tell us which bits are God speaking. "*All* Scripture is breathed out by God and profitable for teaching, for reproof, for correction, and for training in righteousness" (2 Tim 3:16) so none of us is left guessing about God's will for our lives or his demands for obedience from us.

This does not mean we can lift out every command of Scripture and instantly apply it to our lives; there is always a need for intelligent, informed handling and application of God's word. But it is a giant leap from this realization to one that says certain instructions in the New Testament demand conduct from believers that is contrary to God's designs for human relationships.

So then, what is the difference between slavery and an ordered pattern of relationships in marriage? If instructions were given to slaves in the New Testament and slavery is wrong, how can we know that this is not also the case for the instructions about marriage?

Well, there are several differences between slavery and marriage (you will be pleased to know!).

Firstly, slavery is not commanded or commended in the New Testament—in fact, Paul urges slaves who have the chance to gain their freedom to do so (1 Cor 7:21). Marriage, however, is a lifelong God-effected union that is only to be broken in exceptional circumstances, and even then reluctantly (Matt 19:3-9; 1 Cor 7:12-13). That is, the institution of slavery is tolerated and regulated (e.g. Col 3:22-4:1) and freedom is commended, but the institution of marriage is commended and divorce is (reluctantly) tolerated.

Secondly and more importantly, slavery is never explained or defended with the theological underpinning that is used for the complementary relationships between men and women. Slavery is simply taken as a cultural given. However, as we have seen, as Paul explains gender relationships in marriage and in the church, he looks right back to God's intentions for men and women in Genesis 2 (and to a lesser extent Genesis 3) and the relationships in the Trinity (1 Cor 11:3) and the relationship of Christ and the church (Eph 5:25). All these reasons transcend culture. They are not bound to any particular time or place or culture.

And although Peter does not use the same theological under-pinning here in 1 Peter 3, the reasons he gives for the different responsibilities of wives and husbands are not the cultural expectations of non-believing husbands or Christian wives, or even the cultural expectations of Graeco-Roman antiquity.

His reasons are that wifely submission is "for the Lord's sake" (2:13); that it is very precious to God (3:4); that this is the way women who hope in God have always lived and made themselves beautiful (v. 5); that it is an expression of a wife doing "good" (v. 6; cf. 2:14, 15, 20; 3:12, 17; 4:19); and that a husband's considerate and respectful leadership of his wife has a direct impact on his spiritual wellbeing (v. 7; cf. v. 12).

Clearly, none of these can be dismissed as obviously cultural. So Peter's instructions for Christian wives and husbands have not passed their use-by date just because they are mentioned alongside the outdated practice of slavery.

2. For mixed-faith marriages only

A second objection is a variation on the first: it is that Peter's instructions apply to Christian wives married to unbelieving husbands (in the first century and/or now), but not within Christian marriages. This argument claims that Peter does not want the freedoms that come with the gospel to unsettle domestic relationships. So while believing spouses are to have equal and identically reciprocal roles and responsibilities, the Christian wife of an unbelieving husband is to limit the expression of her freedom and still operate within the culturally mandated ordered pattern of relationships.

Because this view is a variation of the cultural argument that we have just looked at—except that it operates at the level of the husband and wife instead of the culture as a whole—the observations made above about counter-cultural Christian conduct apply here too.

But also, as we have seen, the call for Christian wives to submit to their husbands is not limited to mixed-faith marriages. It is found in Paul's letters where husbands are believers (Eph 5:22-33; Col 3:18-19; Titus 2:5; cf. 1 Cor 14:34-35; 1 Tim 2:11-12). It is embedded in the pattern of marriage God established in the garden of Eden. It reflects the relationship of Christ and the church. And in 1 Peter 3, the mention of the godly women of the past (especially Sarah) prevents these instructions being restricted to wives with unbelieving husbands.

No doubt there are things that a Christian wife with a believing husband will do differently from her Christian sisters who are married to unbelievers; but her need to submit voluntarily and intelligently to her husband does not disappear.

What this passage means for us today

1. For wives married to a believer or planning to marry a believer

So what does this mean for those women married to a believer? Are there ten easy steps to follow?

I wish there were. I said earlier that Peter does not give us much detail about how wifely submission works out in the day to day. Perhaps that is because he was writing to a culture that was not as influenced by feminism as ours, and which had established female roles. Perhaps it is also because, in reality, submission has as many expressions as the relationships in which it is expressed.

What Peter does give us is a list of attitudes and behaviours that *accompany* submission. Some of these are equally important for all Christians: humility, gentleness, a heart shaped by moral and ethical purity and reverence for God, trust in God that frees us from anxiety and fear, and a conscious effort to work on inner beauty rather than external charms. But respect and submission to husbands, and obedience when that is required, are particular to wives.

How this works out in practice will be different for each Christian wife, depending on her personality, her husband's personality, their age, life stage, circumstances and so on. The externals will be different, but the inner attitudes will be the same.

It may be too that this is more observable in the breach than in the fulfilment. We can easily see when submission is not happening, but it is perhaps harder to pinpoint when it *is*.

And the sad truth is that this side of glory it will never be easy. We are sinners, so wives will always want to control or resist their husband's leadership—whether by nagging or yelling or manipulating or undercutting, by using the kids in an emotional tug of war, by gossiping about his failings to their mothers or friends, by overspending his/their money, or by treating him like a child with patronizing condescension. How many husbands feel like they are treated like teenage sons rather than the head of the household!

Sin will take whatever form it can to set a wife against her husband's leadership. That is why wifely submission requires intelligence and wisdom, decisions and diligence, spiritual discernment and plenty of repentance.

It is a life's work. But as Peter tells us: forget the face creams and hair dyes, forget the dress sales; if a wife wants her husband to think she is beautiful, this is where real beauty is found and, better still, it is (God-willing) beauty that improves with time.

2. For those married to an unbeliever

Perhaps the situation Peter sets out is your situation. Perhaps you are a wife with an unbelieving husband. What does this passage mean for you? It means: take heart. Peter (and God, whose word it is) recognizes here that the heart's desire of a Christian wife is for her husband to be saved, and that life in a mixed-faith marriage might not be easy.

Such a woman is living between two worlds. In reality she is a stranger and alien in this world because her real home is with Christ, but she also shares a home and a family with someone who is yet to come to Christ. She may experience ridicule or resistance, and over the years her faith may have become a 'no-go' zone because her husband has read every book, met every Christian friend and heard every evangelistic speaker, and the time for talking is finished. It may be that the only evangelistic option left is of the wordless variety—but don't think that because he is not listening, he is not watching!

To this Christian woman and all who are like her, the living God says: put your hope in me.

She is to concentrate on making herself beautiful in God's sight and not give way to fear. God has her in this marriage for her good and for the good of the whole family. *He* sees what the marriage is like; *he* appreciates the beauty her unbelieving husband may not appreciate. She can put her hope in God—as did the women of old—and he will care for her and use her for his glory. Like her sisters with believing husbands, she is to fear God and he will give her nothing to fear.

3. For Christian husbands

Of course, today there are Christian husbands with unbelieving wives too. They also live between two worlds, with the disappointment and grief of not being able to share their deepest beliefs and hopes with their spouse. They also have an urgent and godly concern for their spouse's eternal destiny.

The task for these Christian husbands is also to conduct themselves in their marriage in such a way as to persuade their wife of the truth of Christ; to speak the words of the gospel as they have opportunity, and to live lives that are a constant witness and compelling demonstration of the truth of the gospel and the power of the cross.

In his brief instructions to husbands, however, Peter expects that they will have Christian wives. And as we finish with 1 Peter 3, there are three questions this passage presents to them.

Firstly: by what criteria do you judge your wife's beauty? It is no secret that a woman's external beauty suffers from the law of diminishing returns. And, no matter how beautiful she is, there will always be women who are more beautiful than her. This is no excuse for a wife to 'let herself go' (there is nothing particularly spiritual about neglecting your physical appearance), but a husband's eyes are to be more attuned to the beauty God creates and desires in her heart than to the sort his eyes can see.

Secondly: would you say you live with your wife in a way that is thoughtful and considerate, that gives her honour and dignity, and is mindful that she is vulnerable to the quality of your leadership? I trust this needs little by way of explanation.

And finally, is the way you relate to your wife a *help* to your prayers? I suspect for each husband this will mean different things, but it is clear from 1 Peter 3 that there is a connection between the two, and so this is a question that no Christian husband can risk not asking himself.

7 | THE ORIGINAL MAN AND WOMAN: GENESIS 1-3

HAVE YOU NOTICED THE recent rash of dancing shows and movies? Movies like *Shall We Dance?*, *Billy Elliott*, *Take the Lead* and *The Full Monty*, and a host of reality TV shows like *Strictly Dancing*, *Dancing with the Stars* and *So You Think You Can Dance*... It seems we cannot get enough of dancing. Together with 'foodtainment', the people making our entertainment must think they are on a winner. And the ratings are proving them right!

Let me say I have the greatest respect for anyone who dances in front of a crowd or camera because when it comes to dancing, I do not think I can dance. I *know* I can't—which is probably why I am spellbound when people *can*. When it is done well, when the man and woman find this amazing harmony and unity, when he leads and she follows and they move as one, floating across the floor twirling and spinning, when it looks effortless... it is exhilarating! It's a few moments of escape from the humdrum.

But those moments are rare and short-lived. Anyone who has ever been to a wedding has seen moments on dance floors they would rather forget—moments that are excruciating rather than sublime, where he goes one way and she goes the other, or where they are doing the right steps but moving stiffly and awkwardly, having to think about every move. In fact, their attempts only go to show how much training and effort are needed to make dancing *seem* effortless!

In this chapter we come to the creation of man and woman and the beginnings of their relationship—to a time when their relationship was effortless, with no awkward movements, no clunky bits, no arguments over who should lead. We come to that time before effortless relations between men and women specifically, and between people generally, became a thing of the past.

This chapter also brings us to the dreadful rejection of God's rule that made these effortless relations a thing of the past. When the dance became excruciating rather than sublime.

The journey so far

I am referring to Genesis 1-3, of course. You will be aware that this is not the first time we have encountered this part of God's living word. In fact, of the passages we have looked at so far, all but one have given us glimpses of Genesis:

- Ephesians 5:31 quotes Genesis 2:24.
- 1 Corinthians 11:7-9 is based on parts of Genesis 1 and 2.
- 1 Timothy 2:13-14 points to parts of Genesis 2 and 3.
- 1 Corinthians 14:34 mentions "the Law" (cf. 1 Cor 14:21) and builds on 11:7-9.

These brief glimpses of Adam and Eve have been like the tip of an iceberg that has bobbed up above the surface into the New Testament and shaped discussions about marriage and ministry. But like all icebergs, there is much more to it than the little bit that floats above the water line.

So now that we have looked at the main New Testament texts that deal directly with the relationships and roles of men and women, we are going back to the beginning of our Bibles to look at what the New Testament assumes. These early chapters of Genesis will give us a better understanding of God's good and perfect intentions for women and men. They will also explain why our experience of gender relationships is so often something other than good and perfect!

But let me make two caveats before we start. First, there is much more to these chapters than what they say about men and women. My hope is that this selective study will prompt you to read all three chapters so you do not miss out on all the other wonderful things they tell us about God, and his creation. And second, I apologize for the speed at which we are going to travel. In a book this short and with texts so long, the sad fact is that we only get to scratch the surface. It is a bit like a Contiki tour of Europe: fast, selective, covering a lot of territory and, hopefully, whetting your appetite to return and do the whole thing more slowly and more thoroughly in the future.

Up close and personal...

You will be aware that there are two creation accounts in the first two chapters of the Bible, which give us two perspectives of the same events. Genesis 1 is like a prologue that gives the big sweeping picture. The second account, beginning at 2:4, is much more detailed. It is the first of eleven family histories in Genesis, but instead of the family history of Adam or Noah, this is the family history of the earth and the heavens (5:1; 6:9; 10:1; 11:10, 27; 25:12, 19; 36:1, 9; 37:2).

When we look at these two accounts we see there is sameness and difference. They are not conflicting accounts, but they are not carbon copies either. Each makes its own distinctive contribution. Each account teaches us the same and different things about God, creation and humankind. Where the first is concerned with the origins of creation and God's relationship with his creation, the second is concerned with relationships within God's creation and the origins of evil. The two accounts are like two sides of the same coin, and we need both sides. Together they help us know who God is and who we are.

And because what we learn about God provides the context for what we learn about ourselves (and because what we learn about God is so wonderful!), we are going to begin by looking at what these chapters tell us about God.

...with God

Not surprisingly, since it occurs within one divinely inspired text of Scripture, the God we meet in Genesis 2 is the same God we meet in Genesis 1.

He is the sovereign ruler over all creation. He is the main actor on the stage. He is there before anything else exists. He is a God who acts. He decides what will happen and then makes it happen. He creates order from formlessness and chaos. He provides good things to meet all the needs of those he has made (1:29; 2:9, 16). He is generous and kind. He is a speaking God, who can be known and who deliberates at a critical juncture in the creation of humanity (1:26, 2:18). He is the ruler and lawgiver, who speaks to and commands those he has made (1:28, 2:16-17). He entrusts humanity with the care of his creation (1:28, 2:15).

But the two accounts also show us different aspects of God's character.

Perhaps the most obvious is his name. In the first account, he is "God". In the second, he is "the LORD God".

In our Bibles generally, and here in Genesis 2 (and 3), the word 'LORD' is written with small capital letters to show that the special Hebrew name for God, YHWH (Yahweh), was used in the original language. So in chapter 2, we have a combination of the *general* name for God (used in chapter 1), and the *personal* name for God— YHWH, the name associated with God's covenant with Israel.

The God we meet in the first account is the mighty creating God of all creation and all people—as his name suggests. It points to his universal rule. But Genesis 2 tells us that this mighty God is also a personal God, who enters into relationship with his people, reveals himself to them, dwells with them, and commits himself to them—as his name suggests. And the name change in chapter 2 to "LORD God" emphasizes this intimate presence with and commitment to those he has made.

The picture of God in each account corresponds with this change in emphasis. In chapter 1 we see God's transcendence, vastness and power, and his separateness from his creation (hence the need to make mankind in his image as his representative in creation). Here he speaks and sees—he announces, commands, executes, approves, and names the ordered developments of his new creation. In chapter 2, it is God's immanence or presence that we notice. He *sends* rain. He *shapes* man from dust like a potter working with clay, and *breathes* life into his nostrils. He *plants* a garden into which he *puts* the man. He *forms* the animals from dust. He *makes* woman by causing the man to fall into a deep sleep and by *taking* a rib and *closing up* the flesh and then *forming* the woman before *bringing* her to the man, like a father presenting his daughter at her wedding.

That is, this is not Bette Midler's remote God watching us from a distance, but a God who is up-close-and-personal. He walks in the garden—he is present in his creation (3:8). He touches it. Breathes into it. Forms it like a master potter and surgeon. As his name shows, this LORD God, our God, is a personal God who involves himself and commits himself to what he has made.

And so, despite his otherness, the God we meet in Genesis 1 and 2 is a God we can know. He is both transcendent and immanent: far above and beyond us but also with us and close to us. He is the all-sovereign, all-powerful, almighty God, who visits his people and is present with them. Here. Now. Always.

...with creation

And just as there are similarities and differences between these two creation accounts in their portrayal of God, the two pictures of creation also have sameness and difference.

There are some important similarities. In both accounts, chaos and formlessness are replaced by order and distinction, purpose and productivity. Notably, naming is an important part of the ordering of God's creation in each account.

In both accounts, creation is totally separate from God. He is present, but he is not part of creation. There is no pantheistic 'green' theology, where creation *is* God or contains God. Neither is there a panentheistic *Avatar* theology where creation is part of God or infused by God. No. There is one God who creates everything, and he is entirely separate from it.

But there are also differences in the portrayal of creation. Genesis 1 gives us the 'Google Earth' view of the whole world, where we see every aspect of creation in its broad array. Genesis 2 on the other hand gives us the 'street view' where we can see street names (or in this case, the names of rivers and lands), the neighbouring localities, the fruit on the trees and even the inhabitants walking around.

The picture we get at street level is one of abundance. It is a place of 'delight', which is what 'Eden' means. It is paradise. Even the gold is particularly good (v. 12), and the trees are not only good for food; they are beautiful, too (v. 9).

Of course, this tells us something about what God is like. He did not cobble together a half-good creation, but lavished upon it his goodness and wisdom and care.

And this generous, personal and present God who created each one of us is the God we need to know and trust as we consider the relationships of women and men. He is good. He knows us. He wants what is best for us. We are not being asked to obey a

God we do not know or whose wisdom we cannot trust or whose nature is not love.

As we think about gender, our battle is to resist allowing what we know from bitter human experience to drown out what we know about the holy God of love.

...with humanity

When it comes to humanity, we can immediately see obvious similarities between the two accounts. Humankind is the pinnacle of creation in both. The creation of humans is introduced by divine speech. Their creation and role are the high points of each account. And in each, humans are to rule and benefit from the world that God has generously created and entrusted to them.

But there are also differences. In Genesis 1, humanity's resemblance to God is at the fore—being made in his image and likeness, to rule. In Genesis 2 it is man's resemblance to the animals that is most evident: he (that is, *male* man) is formed out of the dust, just as they are (vv. 7, 19; cf. 3:19). This means that whereas in chapter 1 God is our closest kin, in chapter 2 our closest kin is the animals. So we have an exalted view of humanity, and then a humble one. We are both magnificent and dust. Like God, and yet also one of his creatures.

But there is an even more obvious difference between what God teaches us about humanity in each chapter. In chapter 1, while we are told that "man" is created "male and female" (v. 27), the differences between male and female are not jumping off the page. But they are in Genesis 2.

A few years ago, I had a non-Christian lady in my Bible study group who was enjoying Bible study so much that she thought she would start reading the Bible with her eight-year-old daughter.

As you do when you read most books, she started at the very beginning. But by the end of these first chapters of Genesis, as someone raised on feminism and the belief that men and women have to be the same to be equal, she was so outraged by what she read that she slammed the Bible shut and vowed never to read it again because it was so sexist.

Now in most ways I think she misunderstood what she was reading, but in one respect she understood what some Christian feminists try to ignore, which is that there *is* a difference between the man and woman in these chapters, both in their responsibilities and in the order of their relationship. And this difference speaks right to the heart of God's design for us even to this day.

To get a good look at these God-given similarities and differences, we need to slow our Contiki tour right down so that we can get a good look at the scenery as we drive by. We will begin this closer look with the account in Genesis 1.

Genesis 1: Male and female

There are several signposts in Genesis 1 pointing to the fact that God's creative activity reached a climax with the creation of humanity, and that human beings are significantly different from all the other creatures of God's creation.

For example, when God creates humankind, it is the first time he thinks out loud about his creative activity—not "Let there be" but "Let us make" (v. 26). It is also the first time God creates something with a direct correspondence to himself—in his image and likeness, related primarily to him. And it is the first time that his presence in his creation is to be physically represented.

Humankind is not the next evolutionary step up from the apes, but an entirely new creature with an entirely unique purpose. No matter what we make of the relationship between the early chapters of Genesis and the actual beginnings of creation, science must not distract us from the absolute uniqueness of humanity in creation *and* in God's purposes.

And Genesis 1:27 makes this uniqueness quite clear:

- Line 1: So *God created man* in his own image,
- Line 2: *in the image of God* he created him;
- Line 3: *male and female* he created *them.*

Although at first glance it seems that each of these lines is saying the same thing, on closer inspection each line is saying something similar but also something different from the others.

In line 1 the emphasis falls on the fact that we are *made by God.* He is our Creator. He made us all. We are his creatures, whoever we are, and we all relate to him as our Creator.

The second line is similar but the emphasis falls on the *image of God* aspect of each person. Line 1 answers the question "Who made man?" Line 2 answers the question "What did God make man like?" And the answer is that he made each one to be like him, to represent him.

Humankind, without exception, is made in the image of God. Men, women, children, different races, different stages of human development, different intelligence, differing capabilities... all human life has been made in the image of God and none bears God's image more than another.

Which brings us to line 3. In lines 1 and 2, man has been spoken of as "man" or "him". But here he becomes "them". It is as if the "him" of line 2 has been hyperlinked, and by clicking on the link you discover that "him" is "them" and they are "male and female".

God created "man" or humanity in two kinds: male and female. Of course, he also created the fish, birds and most other creatures as male and female too. But their sexual differentiation is not mentioned even though some are explicitly told to reproduce, and you don't need pet rabbits to know that God's creatures have been reproducing ever since (v. 22; cf. vv. 21-25). Genesis simply leaves us to assume their sexual nature.

Not so with man and woman. Their differentiation *is* mentioned because it is significant for what it means to be human. It helps tell us who we are.

Not only does the introduction of gender here pave the way for the blessing and command to be fruitful and multiply—essential for our ability to extend God's rule in his creation (v. 28)—but our sexual differences are also part of us being made in the *image of God*. We can see this in the differences between lines 2 and 3, where "in the image of God" is replaced by "male and female", and "him" is replaced by "them".

This is not to say that God is male and female. God is spirit (John 4:24). He does not have gender as we have gender—although, of course, he has revealed himself to us as Father, Son, and Spirit of the Father and the Son, and we must relate to God in light of his self-revelation.

Rather, it suggests that one aspect of the image of God in humanity is the unity, compatibility, and complementarity of these two similar but different beings. They are both rightly described as "man", but they are either male or female, and the way these two non-identical halves of humanity relate together to make one people is part of being created in the image of God.

The Bible teaches us that there is one God, but within the one Godhead there are three persons in perfect unity: God the Father, God the Son and God the Holy Spirit. And with the wisdom of New Testament hindsight, we may even get a glimpse of this when God says, "Let *us* make man in *our* image" (Gen 1:26; cf. v. 2)—although it may have escaped the notice of the original author!

And as there is this simultaneous differentiation and unity of persons within the Godhead, so also, before our sin fractured the harmony, there was male and female in perfect unity as the one humanity.

You will recall from chapter 3 of this book that 1 Corinthians 11 gives us another glimpse of this correspondence between the divine relationships and gendered human relationships, when Paul sees that the ideal relationship between a man and a woman reflects the relations within the eternal Godhead.[1]

As it happens, I do think there is more to being made in God's image than just this unity and diversity. There is our role as God's representative rulers of creation, as his face towards all he has made. There is our moral judgement and wisdom, and our capacity for relationships and creativity. But part of being made in the image of God—whatever our age and whether we are married or unmarried—is that we are made for gendered relationships of unity and complementarity.

Now although this account in Genesis 1 emphasizes the sameness of men and women (in that both are made in the image of God with responsibilities to fill the earth and rule over it, and also that 'male' and 'female' are adjectives describing the same humanity), they are at the same time obviously and distinctively different. One is male and one is female, and the differences are *essential* to who they are—not coincidental.

This strikes at the very heart of some feminist thought and at the justification and normalizing of homosexuality that is so prevalent today. It is not as if God made 'persons' who just happen to have male or female external cladding, so that who we are is in no way determined by our gender, and whom we have sex with does not matter so long as they are a (consenting) *person*. This will not do. God made us with sexual polarity, as either male or female.[2] We cannot divorce who we are from our gender. We are not genderless 'persons'. We are *male* or *female* persons, made for differing relationships with people of either the same gender as ours or the opposite of ours. Because of this, whether we are

---

1   "…the head of the woman is man, and the head of Christ is God" (1 Cor 11:3, NIV).

2   This does not deny the existence of individuals with ambiguous physiological gender. These rare disorders, as with all other physical frailty and suffering, are tragic evidence of the disruption and distortion of God's good purposes brought about by human rebellion. While these individuals are fully made in the image of God and equally created and loved by him, these disorders were not part of God's original design for humanity.

married or unmarried and in every relationship in which we find ourselves, our gender matters. It is a fixed part of our identity. It is not a role we put on and take off or only need for marriage or procreation.

Our gender is inseparable from who we are.

Moreover, it is clear that, as male and female, man and woman need each other. They are charged with filling the earth and subduing it, and simple biology tells us they cannot do that alone (as Paul says in 1 Corinthians 11:11-12). Their mission is a joint calling that requires and arises from their sexual differences, and they need each other to do what God created and designed them to do.

And before we leave this first account we must notice that creation is now *very* good (Gen 1:31). With the arrival in God's creation of man, as male and female made in the image of God, the pinnacle is reached and so "on the seventh day God finished his work that he had done, and he rested on the seventh day from all his work that he had done" (2:2).

Genesis 2: The man and the woman

First God made the man

Now whereas Genesis 1 took us through the orderly progressive steps and days of God's work of creation, Genesis 2 lands us with a thud in the middle of the sixth day (v. 7). It is concerned not so much with the whole created order but with the relationships within God's creation, and how the blessing and command of the sixth day will be worked out in practice (cf. 1:28). And central to that question is the creation and relationships of God's image bearers.

So what can we learn about humanity in Genesis 2?

First, we see that the man is clearly created first. His first mention is at 2:7 where he is made from the dust of the ground. And we are told twice that God put him into the garden (vv. 8, 15). Man is the first character God places on the stage, and throughout the chapter he remains centre stage (apart from God, that is).

Moreover, even before God mentions the need for the woman, he gives the task of working and caring for the garden directly to the man (v. 15). So, too, with the formal statement of God's covenant with humanity: God speaks directly to the man (vv. 16-17).

And there are two corresponding parts of God's command. The man is told he is free to eat from every tree in the garden— to eat freely from every one of those magnificent trees, including the tree of life. But there is a condition, a limit to his freedom: he must not eat of "the tree of the knowledge of good and evil". Doing so will bring certain death—so this prohibition is for his own good, and an expression of God's goodness.

But then this idyllic picture is shattered with God's verdict of his creation. Something is *not* good: "It is *not* good that the man should be alone" (v. 18). Now, this should hit us like a freight train. All along, God's verdict has been "good", "good", "good" and "very good" (1:4, 10, 12, 18, 21, 25, 31; 2:9, 12). The picture thus far has been one of perfect order and superabundance!

But something is missing. And not only is God's creation missing something good; there is a *gaping hole*. The man is alone and it is not good. And so God announces he will make "a helper fit for him" (2:18). God will meet the man's need.

But not immediately. First, all the animals God has created are brought to the man for him to name. But although they too are made from dust, none of them is right. No suitable helper is found (v. 20). At the end of all his naming activity, the man is still alone and it is still not good.

Then God made the woman

So "the LORD God caused a deep sleep to fall upon the man, and while he slept took one of his ribs and … made [it] into a woman and brought her to the man" (vv. 21-22). The man recognizes her as his other half, and with delight exclaims, "This at last is bone of my bones and flesh of my flesh; she shall be called Woman, because she was taken out of Man" (v. 23). This is what he has been looking for but did not (and could not) find among the animals. He recognizes her as God's answer to his aloneness.

What a climax this is, and all the more so because it is the first human speech recorded in the Bible. It is a speech of delight about God's good provision in the creation of woman, and the man's recognition of their sameness and difference.

She is like him in that she is made of the same stuff as him: the same bone, the same flesh—she is his kin (Gen 29:14; Judg 9:2; 2 Sam 5:1). She is *like* him but she is not *identical* to him. She is something different. His aloneness hasn't been resolved with someone identical to him (another man), or with something foreign to him (an animal), but with someone essentially like him but opposite to him. His other half. His complement.

Now I don't know what you make of it being a rib. The 17th-century English minister Matthew Henry suggested the woman was "not made out of his head to rule over him, nor out of his feet to be trampled upon by him, but out of his side to be equal with him, under his arm to be protected, and near his heart to be beloved".[3] I admit that it's a bit corny, and of course it is poetic licence not Scripture. But I think he has captured the sentiment even if he is guilty of a little eisegesis!

Whatever you make of the rib, it is because of their similarity and difference that when a man and woman join together in marriage, they become one (Gen 2:24). It is the *re*union of two halves. Marriage is not two identical people being joined together (as the homosexuals wish). It is two different but similar and complementary beings coming together as *one flesh*: one flesh in their sexual union, one flesh in the children they produce, one in

---

3   M Henry, *Commentary on the Whole Bible Volume 1: Genesis to Deuteronomy*, Christian Classics Ethereal Library, Grand Rapids, 2000 (1706), p. 41.

their spiritual and emotional bond, and one flesh as a new social entity, a new family relationship that supersedes all previous ties.

Which brings us to the end of the chapter, where we leave our happy couple in the garden, basking in the sunshine, naked and unconcerned, delighting in each other and in the limitless wisdom and generosity of their Creator.

...and they danced!

Before we move on, let us take a closer look at their relationship. It is one of equality and difference. Their equality is plain enough. It was plain in Genesis 1 where they were both made in the image of God, and it is plain here as well. Here, they are both made of the same flesh and bone. They are both formed by God. They both inhabit the garden and enjoy God's provision. They are both bound by the same divine commands.

But here in Genesis 2 the differences between the man and woman become more obvious—and, in fact, it is these differences upon which the New Testament draws when it discusses the roles and relationships of men and women in marriage and in Christian fellowship.

Here in Genesis these differences show there is an order in the relationship. The man and woman are equals but they are not identical, either in appearance (which is not explicit in the text) or in role (which is). He has a responsibility of leadership that she does not have, and she has a responsibility that he does not have, which is to accept his leadership and help tend and keep the garden.

This ordered relationship is evident at several points.

It is seen in him being the firstborn. He is formed first and is first in the garden. The woman, on the other hand, is made after him. That is, he has *temporal* priority. He is born first.

In Western cultures being the firstborn is not usually a big deal, so we can easily miss its significance here. But in ancient cultures, as in some cultures today, the firstborn has responsibilities of leadership and authority, and we see this with the man in Genesis 2. God gives the command to him (vv. 16-17). The man names the animals (v. 20) and he also names the woman (v. 23; also 3:20). These are all aspects of Adam's rule as firstborn in God's creation.

And the apostle Paul points to this temporal priority to explain his instructions about ordered relationships between men and women in church. In 1 Timothy 2 it is one of two reasons why women are not to teach or have authority over men, and in 1 Corinthians 11:8 the fact that "man was not made from woman, but woman from man" is one of several reasons Paul gives for gender-distinctive conduct when believers pray and prophesy in church.

But Adam's firstborn-ness is not the only sign of this ordered relationship; there is also the difference in the tasks God assigns to the man and the woman. She is made as "a helper fit for him" (not the other way around). As Paul puts it: "Neither was man created for woman, but woman for man" (1 Cor 11:9).

Unless you have been living in a cultural bubble for decades, you will feel the jarring strangeness and even offence of God's word at this point—especially if you are a woman. It is completely contrary to the feminist values that rule Western cultures, and to our sinful nature that wants always to be number one, and it runs in the face of our experience of male authority (and the abuse of it) in our post-Genesis-3 world. This means we are battling on three fronts to see how this divine design of ordered relationships could possibly be a good thing.

But God is asking us to put all that aside and to hear his word; to see how good things were before human sin messed them up. And the first step in doing that is to realize that the word 'helper' is not a put-down.

Woman is not 'helper' in the way that a child might be 'mummy's little helper'. Nor is she 'helper' in the sense that men are CEOs who really get things done and women are just nameless junior office hacks and eye-candy, only ever undeserving second-class citizens in God's kingdom.

In fact, in the Old Testament this word 'helper' is most often used of God. God's people can declare that the Lord is "our help and our shield" (Ps 33:20) and that "The LORD is on my side as my helper" (Ps 118:7). God is not above being a helper.

And when he helps, he takes on a supportive or serving role to those he is helping without ever ceasing to be the sovereign Lord of all. He provides what is lacking so that the one he is helping can complete their task.

What we discover when we look at the Old Testament's use of this word is that 'helper' is not a term of value or worth. It is a *type of relationship*.

The woman is created for a relationship in which she is a helper fit for the man. She is not to help the animals. In fact she is not even to help God. She is to be a helper for the man. And she does that by solving his aloneness (remember, it was "not good" that he was alone). With her creation comes the creation of human community, and the ability to be fruitful and multiply and together fill the earth and tend it as God commanded them both (Gen 1:28).

The ordered relationship between the man and woman then is seen in his firstborn-ness and in her role as "a helper fit for him". It is also seen in the name he gives her (2:23), and in his initiating role in establishing a new family (v. 24). In short, he has a God-given responsibility to lead and she has a God-given responsibility to accept his leadership, and together they form a partnership.

But while they have different responsibilities, there is no inequality between them. Genesis 2 is no excuse for men thinking they are better than women (or vice versa!). Men and women may be different but it is not a difference of superiority and inferiority.

As one writer puts it: this is not the march of patriarchalism (where the man hammers out the beat) or the race of feminism (where the woman wins), but rather the man and woman are equal and with different responsibilities. In God's good design, their relationship is neither a march nor a race, but a *dance* where the man leads and the woman follows, and yet together they move as one, in perfect harmony.[4]

As the New Testament writers make plain, and as we have seen in the earlier chapters of this book, this dance is God's design not only for Eden, but also for New Testament times and for the present day—in the headship of a husband and submission of a wife in marriage (Ephesians 5; Colossians 3; Titus 2; 1 Peter 3), and in male leadership and teaching of the church family (1 Corinthians 11 and 14; 1 Timothy 2).

This is the dance for all of us today if we consider ourselves Christians.

Genesis 3: The elephant in the room

But of course it is no longer as simple as putting on the music and taking to the dance floor. There is a crippling obstacle in the way: sin. Which brings us to Genesis 3.

There, in this Eden God has created, the devil in the form of a serpent uses God's own words to incite rebellion.[5] It asks the woman "Did God *actually* say, 'You shall not eat of *any* tree in the garden'?" (v. 1)—subtly twisting God's words, which were heavy on generosity and light on prohibition (2:16-17). But instead of replying to the serpent's closed question with a simple "No", the woman replies with her own subtle twisting and misquoting of God's words: "...'neither shall you *touch it*, lest you die'" (3:3).

---

4   D Bloesch, 'Donald Bloesch Responds', in *Evangelical Theology in Transition: Theologians in Dialogue with Donald Bloesch*, ed. EM Colyer, IVP, Downers Grove, 1999, p. 207.
5   For texts that identify the serpent with the devil/Satan, see Revelation 12:9, 20:2; 2 Corinthians 11:3-4, cf. 2:11, 11:14; and, more obliquely, the connection between Jesus' victory over Satan and the authority he gave his disciples over snakes in Luke 10:18-20.

'Not so—you will not die', responds the serpent. Then, having planted the seed of doubt in her mind about the truthfulness and goodness of God's word, the serpent tells half-truths, promising that if she follows its advice, her eyes will be opened, and she will be "like God, knowing good and evil" (v. 5).

And so the woman saw and took and ate (v. 6). And she gave some to her husband and he ate.

It is no accident, I take it, that the serpent chooses to talk to the woman rather than to the man. What this temptation represents, step by step, is the total reversal of God's created order of relationships. The man is to submit himself to the command of God (as is the woman), the woman is to accept the leadership of the man, and the man and woman together are to have authority over the creatures. But all of that is turned on its head.

Instead, the creature leads the woman, the woman leads the man, and together they doubt and disobey the good word of God and instead seek to be like him (which they are *already*!). Put another way: the woman listens to the creature, the man listens to the woman, and neither of them listens to God.

The narrative focuses us on this reversal of God's order at five points.

First, the climax or pivot of the account in the original text is the words: "and he ate" (v. 6). It is at this point that the reversal, the final fatal step had been taken.

Second, when the Lord God responds to their sin it is the man that he calls to account (v. 9), thereby reasserting the original created order.

Third, when Adam is judged he is judged not only because he ate from the tree but also because he listened to his wife (v. 17). That is, Adam did two things wrong. He disobeyed God by eating the very fruit he was told not to eat, *and* he disobeyed God by listening to his wife and ignoring his God-given responsibility to lead her (rather than follow). She might have been deceived (v. 13), but he was not (cf. 1 Tim 2:14).

Fourth, the death sentence in 3:19, which is the fulfilment of the threat in 2:17, is directed at the man, and its language takes us right back to the creation of man from the dust at the beginning of the second account (cf. 2:7). He is still the firstborn who learns first that he will die.

And fifth, in a related point, Adam functions as the head of humanity. It is because of Adam's sin that the creation is cursed (3:17), and the death sentence passed on him will also be passed on all those related to him (vv. 22-24).

But even before God declares his response (v. 14), the consequences of his creatures' rebellion are painfully clear. The wonderful picture of harmony between God and his creation, between man and woman, between God and humanity, and between mankind and creation has been lost. Every relationship is affected.

God, who to this point has been revealed as the loving, generous, all-powerful, all-wise life-giver and lawgiver, is now revealed also as judge and deliverer.

Up until now the creation had reflected its Creator's will. Each part had its place in relationships of order determined by the word of God. But in the Fall, his word and his order are rejected and so he becomes the judge of creation. That is why Adam and Eve instinctively hide from him in the garden (v. 8).

But God is also the gracious deliverer. He has not rejected his creation. He is still present. He still talks with the man and his wife. He still loves them, so he curses the serpent and promises that one day the woman's offspring will bruise its head (which I take it is a promise about the Lord Jesus Christ, who triumphed forever over evil).

And he still provides for the man and woman: he gives them

clothes (v. 21); he expels them from the garden so they can't eat from the tree of life and live forever as sinners (vv. 22-23); he still provides them with food (vv. 17-18); he blesses them with offspring (v. 20). But, unlike before, the birth of children will be painful (v. 16) and growing food will be hard work (vv. 17-18).

The battle of the sexes

But the damage was not limited to our relationship with God; the relationship between man and woman also changed.

We get a glimpse of this when God confronts Adam as the head of creation. It is apparently God's fault ("The woman whom *you* gave to be with me") and Eve's fault ("*she* gave me fruit")—in fact, anyone's fault but his own (v. 12). She is no longer his complement and companion, but his opponent. Their relationship has been fractured.

This is made clear in the sentence God pronounces against the woman: "Your desire shall be for your husband, and he shall rule over you" (v. 16b). Simple! But what is this desire, and what does this verse mean?

There are several popular explanations that fail to satisfy.

The strangest one I have heard takes it as a woman's sexual desire, so it means that a woman always desires her husband *sexually*, but he rules over her by denying her what she wants. This is usually greeted at women's conferences with muffled laughter—presumably because it belies the usual pattern of desire discrepancy!

Another explanation takes it like the Tammy Wynette song 'Stand By Your Man', where all the little lady wants to do is stick by her man and look after him, but he just takes and takes, taking advantage of her and ruling over her.

But the problem with these two suggestions is that they make men the bad guys and paint women as morally good. But that is not what is being said in Genesis. Both the man and the woman have disobeyed God and both are sinful.

The key to this enigmatic sentence is found in the next chapter of Genesis where the same Hebrew terminology is used for sin's desire for Cain and Cain's need to master it: "...sin is crouching at the door. Its desire is for you, but you must rule over it" (4:7). Sin's desire is to dominate Cain and to control him but he is to master or resist it.

Going back to 3:16, this means that Eve's desire is a desire to dominate or manipulate or control her husband—that she will no longer willingly submit to his headship but will want to rule him instead. He, on the other hand, will rule over her. His headship is not a result of the Fall, but the way he expresses that headship after the Fall is—that is, as domination.

The unity, harmony and teamwork of Genesis 2 has been replaced by woman's constant desire to control her husband, and his loving leadership has been replaced by domination or abdication (which is actually a passive form of domination).

This verse, then, does not represent the *institution* of male headship and wifely submission, but the *distortion* of it. The battle of the sexes has begun.

We only need to look at the rest of the Bible (or at history or our own lives) to know how that battle has played out ever since. Even that battle is only but a part of the devastation that sin has brought to all relationships. Of course, the rest of the Bible also tells us everything our loving and good God has done in response to our sin and predicament, and how we are to live in response to that.

In fact, this is the message of the rest of the Bible—a message glimpsed in Genesis 3 in God's continued relationship with, provision for and deliverance of these original partners in crime, who remain privileged bearers of God's image in his creation (5:1-2, 9:6).

The honeymoon is over

Before we leave Genesis 1-3, and in the context of the counter-cultural things these chapters have to say to us about men and women, it would be remiss not to consider marriage.

In Genesis 2 we meet the first man and first woman. You will probably have noticed that they also happen to be the first husband and wife. When we look at their relationship from that angle, we see that God's intentions for sex and marriage are no less confronting to our culture and our individual sinfulness than his pattern of gender relationships.

Every aspect of God's design for sex and marriage (v. 24) is currently under attack. God's design for marriage could now reasonably be considered the minority view! That design is:

- Marriage is between a man and a woman.
- Marriage establishes a new family that has priority over all previous relational ties and commitments.
- Marriage involves a decisive public cleaving to one another in a lifelong covenant (not shacking up together in a let's-see-how-this-works-out arrangement).
- Marriage creates an exclusive one-flesh union.
- Marriage is very good (it is not a bondage or burden, but a blessing from God).

And because all of us are post-Genesis-3 people living in post-Genesis-3 relationships, some of us will have messed up God's design for sex and marriage. Perhaps we have been sexually active outside marriage. Perhaps we have had a list of sexual partners. Perhaps we are attracted to people of the same sex. Perhaps we are divorced. Perhaps we are married and we want out, or perhaps we have never cut the umbilical cord to our parents.

Genesis 2:24 and the rest of God's word tell us that this is not how God intended marriage to be.

Indeed, even though we might not have done any of these 'big bad' things, none of us is innocent in regards to our sexuality—in its desires and expression (cf. Matt 5:28; Rom 1:24).

But praise be to God (Alleluia!), whose word also tells us that while we may have wandered a very long way from God's intentions, he has given us a very great Saviour, the Lord Jesus Christ—and so whatever we have done against God's good commands for sex and marriage, it is not a death sentence: we can be completely forgiven through Jesus' blood. So if there are things we need to repent of, there is no reason to put it off. In fact there is an urgency to repent, to turn our back on our sin and accept his wonderful forgiveness, and put Christ on the throne of even our most private moments.

Finally, a word to the unmarried: those who have never married, those widowed, and those now divorced. Genesis 2 introduces the first husband and first wife, but it also introduces the first man and first woman. That is, we do not have to be married to experience the good that is on view here.

The man's problem was not singleness. It was *solitude*. He was *alone*, not unmarried.

Sexual differentiation means none of us is alone—as Adam was alone—because we are all in relationships—more than that, we are all in *gendered* relationships. All of us relate to men and women, as parents, siblings, friends, workmates, at church—in fact, everywhere we go. And so, with varying degrees of intimacy, all of us experience the complementarity, the dance, between women and men.

Marriage *is* the most intimate expression of that dance. And so it should be. But none of us is excluded from it. Already in this book we have seen how the New Testament passages about women and men in the church show that all of us in the body of Christ have our part to play in ordered and complementary relationships between women and men.

When you think about it like that, the dance floor becomes a wonderfully crowded space where everyone is welcome and everyone belongs.

8 | THE ULTIMATE DISTORTION

I GUESS WE HAVE ALL HAD experiences when words slip out of our mouths—especially ones intended as a joke—and the moment they are spoken they no longer seem such a good idea. What on earth were we thinking? But the damage is done. All we can do is try to tidy up the mess.

Such was the experience of Australian politician Alexander Downer in 1994, when he jokingly suggested his party's domestic violence policy could be called 'The Things That Batter' as a play on the words of the party's election slogan 'The Things That Matter'. But the joke was lost, not only on those who heard it but on the entire populace as it splashed across newspapers. And for a while it looked as if Alexander Downer's political aspirations were lost too, before he went on to become Australia's longest serving Minister for Foreign Affairs. By then he had learnt his lesson: domestic violence is nothing to joke about.

Neither is it ever justified. But the tragic fact is that there are some men—*not many*, but a few—who (mis)use the Bible texts we have been examining in this book to justify their mistreatment of their wives.

There are also people who reject the proper expression of this biblical teaching, and wrongly accuse Christians who accept it of encouraging and/or condoning domestic abuse of women.

I know this firsthand. Some years ago when I appeared in a national television program about the push for female bishops in Australia, my interlocutor responded to my presentation of the biblical pattern of relationships by saying that it "frightened" her because "it's that sort of talk that has led to generations of domestic violence in the home". I objected to the broadcaster about the inclusion of her accusation as I abhor violence against women (and men, for that matter), but my objections fell on deaf ears.

But this is my book and I am not going to leave the door open for that false accusation to be made again.

And so, regrettably, I need to include this chapter to answer these two misuses of God's word. Regrettably too, it will not be fun to read. Reading about sin and brokenness never is. But God's word has things to say about this particular subject, and only his word will bring real hope and healing where this sin and brokenness are found.

I should make clear at the outset that, unlike the rest of this book where I have some credentials for studying Bible texts, I have no qualifications for addressing this issue beyond what I have learned from life experience, including my work as a nurse and in pastoral ministry.

This chapter is also different from the rest of the book in that it does not focus on just one Bible text. Instead, it is an attempt to bring God's word to bear on expressions of male headship and female submission that by cultural standards—and, more importantly, by God's standards—must not be tolerated in Christian households or in the Christian community, however rare they may be.

This chapter does not provide an exhaustive response. It is a selective treatment of the matter that is intended to allay the fears of those who reject God's pattern of relationships for fear of its distortion, and to prevent the (mis)use of God's word as a cover for evil. There is much more that could be said about the dynamics of all kinds of abuse and about the help available for those dealing with it; but this is not the place.

What is abuse?

To get a feel for what we are dealing with, we first must answer the simple question of "What is abuse?" But perhaps not surprisingly there is no simple answer.

The truth is there is a spectrum of behaviour that should be regarded as 'abuse', just as there is a spectrum of behaviour that we would consider 'acceptable'. And as we move down the abuse spectrum, there is an increasing element of subjectivity about what constitutes abuse. Physical violence (e.g. kicking, choking, beating, using weapons), which is at the high end of the spectrum, has no element of subjectivity. It either happened or did not, and right-thinking people easily recognize it as abuse.

However when we move down the spectrum to, for example, coercion and threats, the abusive nature of the conduct is more dependent on the perception of the victim (but not entirely). This makes it harder for someone outside a relationship to appreciate the destructive and controlling power of coercion and threats within that relationship, because their force rests on the dynamics and history of the relationship. It is also possible that perpetrators might sometimes be victims and victims sometimes perpetrators, even within the same relationship.

This all means that if we are looking for simple and neat definitions and categories, we will not find them. There may be some clear-cut instances of abuse, but often what constitutes abuse will have fuzzy edges that must be understood on a relationship-by-relationship basis. At the very least, we must realize that physical blows are not the only way a person may be cowered into fearful non-voluntary subjection.

Those cautions stated, the spectrum of domestic abuse includes the following:

- Physical assault (e.g. deliberate physical actions causing harm)
- Sexual assault (e.g. non-consensual sexual acts, forced compliance, rape)
- Coercion and threats (e.g. to hurt/remove children, property, pets)
- Intimidation (e.g. looks, gestures or actions threatening violence or loss)
- Isolation and/or social abuse (e.g. loss of freedom, restricted contact with family/friends)
- Psychological/emotional/verbal abuse (e.g. put-downs, criticism, mind-games)
- Economic abuse (e.g. control and/or withholding of family resources)

Sadly, this list is by no means exhaustive. Just as the heart of fallen human beings is hopelessly corrupt and deceitful (Ps 14:1-3; Jer 17:9; Rom 3:9-18), there is no end to the expressions abuse might take. At the same time though, we need to realize that this same fallen human heart can name as abuse conduct that is not abuse: it can make accusations about things that did not happen, and it can (intentionally or unintentionally) perceive and/or depict acceptable behaviour as abuse. This is not to cast doubt on all claims of abuse, but to caution against a quickly reached, one-sided view. It is important that the truth not become a casualty in our attempts to understand or help.

How often does abuse really happen?

The true incidence of domestic abuse is almost impossible to know. Not only are there issues of subjectivity and a spectrum of abuse at play, but the dynamics of abuse also work against accurate statistics. Abuse thrives in an environment of fear-induced and shame-induced silence, which means that much abuse goes unreported. So all the statistics need to be revised upwards, but by how much—God alone knows!

A recent survey conducted by the Australian Bureau of Statistics found that 0.9% of men and 2.1% of women in Australia had experienced actual violence since the age of 15 from a person who was an intimate partner at the time the assault occurred. Of that number, 27% reported that there were children in their care who witnessed the violence. The figures for violence inflicted by a person who was a previous partner at the time of the assault is significantly higher, at 4.9% for men and 15% for women. Violence from a previous partner was more likely to be a one-off incident, whereas current partner abuse was recurrent.[1]

What this survey makes clear, and what is usually overlooked by feminists, women's groups, governments, and those who blame the Bible's ordered pattern of marriage for all domestic abuse, is that intimate partner violence is *not exclusively perpetrated by men*. Indeed, almost one in three victims of intimate partner abuse are male.[2]

What this survey also makes clear is that intimate partner violence is not restricted to any one demographic. It occurs across all socio-economic groups, cultures, races, and geographic regions (with some variations in occurrence). And 20 years in pastoral ministry has convinced me that the Christian community is no exception to this. I have known Christian women abused by their Christian husbands, and Christian men abused by their Christian wives. And while some of these marriages were complementarian by conviction—even where wives were the perpetrators—others espoused an egalitarian model.

---

1   Australian Bureau of Statistics, *Personal Safety Survey Australia*, ABS cat. no. 4906.0, reissued edn, ABS, Belconnen, 2006, p. 11.

2   *Personal Safety Survey Australia*, p. 30. These statistics do not include the male prison population (cf. p. 43).

This shows that the reasons for intimate partner abuse are far more complex than a simple name-and-blame-the-apostle-Paul game can explain, even within Christian marriages. It is a cheap shot. There *may* be a small number of men who twist the biblical teaching so it becomes an excuse for the very conduct it was intended to prevent, but those who blame the biblical teaching for this abuse are not blaming the biblical pattern at all, but a sinful *distortion* of it.

Regrettably though, and whatever the reasons for it, the chances are that if you have been a Christian for any length of time, you know Christian people (men and women) for whom domestic abuse of some kind is a present or past reality. It may be that it is or has been for you. Let me say clearly: it is our Christian duty not to condone or tolerate it—whether in ourselves, in our homes or in our churches.

A pastoral response

The pastoral response to domestic abuse is varied and complex, not least because the nature of abusive relationships is varied and complex. Just as no two relationships are identical, no two situations of abuse are either. And to complicate things further, those offering pastoral care only ever see a part of the relational dynamic and usually only after abusive patterns are well established.

However, I offer the following as *the beginning* of a pastoral response grounded in Scripture.

1. There is no biblical justification for domestic abuse

If you remember nothing else from this chapter, I want you to remember this: there is absolutely no biblical justification or excuse for domestic violence or abuse—against women or men or children. More than that, there are commands against it (Col 3:19; Mal 2:14-16, NIV1984; Prov 11:29).

Paul appears only too aware that some husbands might use their position as a licence to mistreat their wives. His response though, unlike the response of many today, is not to ditch God's original pattern for marriage but to forbid its distortion and command godliness instead. In the same two passages where he instructs wives to submit voluntarily to their husbands, he speaks forcefully to husbands about their responsibilities to their wives. He forbids them being harsh with their wives, and commands them to love their wives as they love their own bodies—nourishing and cherishing them, not hating them (Col 3:19; Eph 5:28-29).

There is no tolerance here of what we might call abuse. Neither is there elsewhere.

And God's word makes plain that physical violence is sin that earns the wrath of God (Pss 11:5-6; 73:3-6, 27; Prov 3:31-32), as does all mistreatment of the vulnerable (Ps 10:2, 8-11, 13-14; Jer 22:3). Scripture gives no justification or solace to those who would get their way through violence or threats of violence. Indeed, the judgement against Israel's leaders for their misuse of authority is a sobering reminder to anyone tempted to use their position of authority for their own benefit (Jer 23:1-4; Ezek 34:2-4).

But it is not just conduct at the high end of the abuse spectrum that God's word names as sin. The destructive words of a should-be friend also deserve his wrath (Ps 55:12-14, 20-21; Matt 5:22), as do fits of rage, bitterness, wrath and malice (Gal 5:19-21; Eph 4:31; Col 3:6-8). Now, no marriage is immune from these sins, simply because all of us are in the process of putting off the old person and putting on the new! But we cannot be complacent if they are found in our homes, especially if they are frequent visitors—and when they *characterize* a relationship, they may well cross the line into abuse.

From the first chapter of the Bible onwards we see that men and women are equally made in God's image with dignity, purpose, moral choice and responsibility, and all of us are individually accountable to God for our conduct (Gen 1:26-28, 2:24, 3:16-19; cf. 1 Cor 7:3). There is no escaping it. We will all answer to God for everything we have done (2 Cor 5:10), and he will judge even those things we have managed to hide from public view (Matt 6:3-4, 6, 17-18; 10:26-31). "I just snapped" or "It just happened" or "She deserved it" are excuses that will never wash with God. Neither will a cycle of abuse followed by remorse—however sincere. But at the same time, God will never leave us alone to fight the temptation to sin. Not only does he give us his in-dwelling Spirit of holiness and the company of others who are tempted as we are, but also he will not let us be tempted beyond our ability to resist or leave us without a better option (1 Cor 10:13).

2. What about turning the other cheek?

Spend any time with people who are living with domestic abuse and before long you will hear Jesus' command to 'turn the other cheek' as a reason to tolerate the abuse. It is true that Jesus said, "But if anyone slaps you on the right cheek, turn to him the other also" (Matt 5:39; Luke 6:29), and it is true that we need to obey his commands. But did he intend these words to be used as a justification for violence? I think not.

Jesus' radical new message is that instead of paying back evil for evil—an eye for an eye—and instead of loving only those who love us, we who follow Jesus are to meet evil with good and love our enemies (1 Pet 3:9; Matt 5:43-47). We are to be extravagantly generous with our love, our possessions, our forgiveness and ourselves, even to those who do not deserve it. We are to do to others as we would have them do to us (Matt 7:12; Luke 6:31).

Shortly we will think about what this might look like, but first it is worth noticing that alongside this instruction of Jesus, Scripture also presents us with a victim's need for justice. For example, Paul and Silas demanded reparation from officials after being severely mistreated in Philippi (Acts 16:35-40); Jesus appealed for justice from the Jewish authorities (John 18:23); and just before his arrest, Jesus told his disciples they could no longer depend on the good will of the people and that they should sell their cloaks to buy a sword (Luke 22:35-36).

These examples warn us against a simplistic 'turn the other cheek' pat answer to domestic abuse. Of course, we *are* to turn the other cheek—but when and how we do that must be informed by the whole of God's word, not a single command in isolation.

3. The command to forgive

Perhaps there can be no better expression of doing to others as we would have them do to us, and returning good for evil, than to forgive someone who has hurt us. Such forgiveness is at the very heart of the gospel, as Christ purchased forgiveness for those who were once his enemies. The testimony of a heart changed by the forgiving power of the cross is that we are able and called to forgive as we ourselves have been forgiven (Mark 11:25; Eph 4:32; Col 3:12-13).

Failure to do so has serious consequences for our salvation. For those who would accept God's forgiveness and yet refuse to forgive those who sin against them, the warnings are chilling, to say the least (Matt 18:21-35)! And this applies to us all, even to the victims of domestic abuse.

But—and it is an important 'but'—that does not mean the abuse must be condoned, excused or tolerated. Here are some reasons why this is so.

Perhaps counter-intuitively, the first reason not to tolerate or excuse abuse is out of *love for the abuser*. The ugly truth about sin is that it is poison to the sinner as well as to the victim (Ps 7:16; Prov 1:11 with 18; Matt 18:15-17; Gal 6:7-8). This means that allowing sin free rein, when it is in our power to restrain it, is not meeting evil with good.

The second reason is out of *love for the other victims* of the abuse. As we saw in the statistics above, children are often present when domestic abuse occurs. This means that even if they are not direct victims—in which case the need to protect them is even more urgent—children are indirect victims. They learn destructive dehumanising behaviour and they learn that solving problems with violence is okay. Their home is a place of anger and fear. They suffer from living with an abused parent—who may be deeply depressed and whose own attitudes and conduct may collude with the abuse—to say nothing of the disruption and distress of hospital visits, police callouts, and the pressure and shame of keeping family secrets.

The third reason is one that involves all of us, not just the immediate victims of abuse. It is that *some domestic abuse is illegal.* One of the few good things to come out of the women's movement in recent decades is that rape within marriage is now recognized as a crime. Other forms of abuse—for example, physical assault, threats, property damage and stalking—are also crimes. This is as it should be. And as Christians we are to obey our governing authorities and the laws of our land (Rom 13:1-4; 1 Pet 2:13-14). This means we are not to do these acts ourselves, and it means we ought not condone or turn a blind eye to them when they occur.

Of course, we can add to this our responsibility as Christians to care for the weak and oppressed, and to be *agents of God's justice* in all the earth. We are not to create our own little domestic haven where we can hide from the evils of the world and leave others to fight their own battles. We are to seek the good of all people, especially our brothers and sisters in the household of faith (Gal 6:10)—whether perpetrators or victims.

Just as we need our spiritual family to check us if we wander into some other sin—greed, gossip, sexual immorality, drunkenness, impatience, pride—those caught in destructive patterns of relating need our help to be free of the sin enslaving them (Gal

6:1). They need our comfort and encouragement. They need our rebuke. They need us to model godly ways of dealing with conflict. And they need us to point them to the Saviour, whose infinite power and authority was displayed on a cross of weakness and shame.

All this being said, we cannot miss the fact that asking victims to forgive their abusers is *a huge ask.*

If it is easier to *say* "I forgive you" than it is to *actually forgive,* it is even easier for one sinner to tell another they must forgive (cf. Mark 2:9-12)! Forgiveness—heartfelt, costly forgiveness—is never easy. For many, this forgiveness will be an ongoing activity involving a lifelong journey of growing in the knowledge and experience of God's grace and learning to extend that grace to a person who, though they promised to love us, has hurt us more than can reasonably be expected in a marriage of two sinners. As I said, forgiveness is not easy. However, by power of the Spirit of God, it is possible.

But we should not confuse forgiving with forgetting.

4. A word about forgiving and forgetting

Many of us have had drummed into us from an early age that the way to resolve conflict is for each side to 'forgive and forget'. It is the sort of advice that allows two warring four-year-olds to bury the hatchet and start playing nicely together again.

This advice works at the time. But fast-forward a few years, and the sorts of things that damage relationships are rarely about who gets to play with the fire engine.

Yet it is hard to shake off that old dictum 'to forgive and forget'. In fact, many of us conflate the two, so that to forgive *is* to forget or to forget *is* to forgive. But the two are quite different.

As we have already seen, it is a requirement of the Christian life that we forgive those who hurt us. I take it that part of forgiveness is not letting a root of bitterness grow up against the person we have forgiven, and not keeping a little black book of wrongs that can be dragged out every time we want to win an argument or guilt someone into giving us our own way. But this is not the same as forgetting. It might be that costly love actually requires us to *remember* some sins.

To give an extreme example: costly love is the sort of love that refuses to put a paedophile on the crèche roster and thereby protects both the children *and* that person—even if that person is sincerely repentant and a full member of our fellowship. This is because (quite apart from child protection laws) our love for that brother or sister means that we *remember* their sin, and do what we can to make the path to righteousness a little easier for them.

Forgiveness of sin does not necessarily mean we are to act as if it never happened.

For similar reasons, while a victim of domestic abuse may have forgiven their spouse and may genuinely want a future for the marriage, it might be wiser for the couple to live apart while the abuser seeks professional and spiritual help to unlearn and change their damaging and destructive ways of relating. The goal of such a separation would be restoration and healing, even if this goal was never realized. Such a step would not be a way of punishing the offender; neither should it be taken lightly or without much prayer and wise Christian counsel.

I realize that what I am suggesting may be controversial and even open to misuse. I realize too that some would recommend the permanent solution of divorce. This is a complex issue that lies well beyond a book of this sort. But it is worth noting that in the Roman world of New Testament times, divorce and remarriage happened easily and often—much like today—and yet Christians were to take quite a different view.

Jesus' and Paul's advice to Christians with troubled marriages was that the door to reconciliation was to be kept open, and the permanent solutions of divorce and remarriage avoided—even when adultery meant that divorce was allowed (1 Cor 7:10-16; cf. Matt 19:3-12). In keeping with this, in situations of abuse separation may be appropriate as a desperate measure for desperate times that provides greater protection to the victims (including children), and which prevents sin and limits further damage to the relationship.

But with or without such desperate measures, God is able to bring restoration and healing. After all, he is the same God who brought dead bones to life before Ezekiel's very eyes (Ezekiel 37). He can do the impossible! This is not a guarantee that he *will*. But we can have strength in knowing that only he *can*.

Practically speaking

It may be that this has been the hardest chapter of this book for you to read. Perhaps you now regret pastoral advice and responses you have given in the past. Perhaps you have looked with new eyes at those sharing the pews with you each Sunday. Perhaps you have been convicted about your own conduct as you have read. Or perhaps it has been hard to see the pages through your tears.

I am only too aware that much more could be said. As I said at the outset, it is the *beginning* of an answer, from a particular angle. It is not the last word!

But as *a* last word to a brief and selective treatment, let me say two final things.

The first is that abusive relationships are often unpredictable and volatile, and 'peace' is often achieved by not rocking the boat. The smallest thing can escalate the situation, and the realization that the secret is out may be enough to disrupt any fragile equilibrium—especially because perpetrators often have a lot invested in outsiders' good opinion of them. So if you have been prompted to respond to a situation, you should know that it is not as simple as turning up on someone's doorstep and telling them to stop what they are doing.

Situations of domestic abuse need to be handled cautiously, wisely, and carefully. If you are a victim, my advice is that you speak to your pastor or to a mature Christian who is preferably the same sex as you. If you are a perpetrator, my advice is the same.

If you are a concerned friend or family member or a pastor who has been asked to intervene then my advice is to act slowly and prayerfully. Make the physical safety of *all those concerned* your first priority (including the perpetrator). Make use of the many resources available for these situations. **Most importantly**, do not *underestimate* the seriousness of the situation or *overestimate* your capacity to deal with it.

The second thing I want to say is this: our society has never been as well equipped to deal with domestic abuse as it is now. There is legislation, policing, scholarship; there are social workers, government and welfare services, crisis shelters, books, support groups; and the list goes on.

As Christians we can be glad of these provisions, yet we would be naïve not to realize that much of this response has been shaped by a feminist agenda that has been slow to see that men can also be victims, and that women can be perpetrators.

And we will be mistaken if we look only to these resources for answers and help. The real problem is a spiritual problem deep in the human heart. It is a problem only God can fix.

So whilst we can and should avail ourselves of the world's resources and the help of professional counsellors and medical personnel—inasmuch as they uphold God's will for humanity and relationships—in the end, it is only the truth of the gospel and the power of the Holy Spirit that can really transform the fallen and broken hearts of men and women.

9 | THE IDEAL WIFE: PROVERBS 31

ENDER STEREOTYPES ARE usually about things that are so self-evident they hardly need pointing out. Little boys like toy trucks and little girls like dolls. Big boys like sport and big girls like shopping. Men like doing and women like talking. Of course, there are always exceptions to the rules, and most stereotypes are gross caricatures. But even then, there is enough truth in them to make them stick.

With that in mind, let me offer a gender stereotype about Proverbs 31:10-31: men *love* it and women *don't*.

When men read Proverbs 31 they are reading about the perfect wife. This is a woman they would like to marry. This is a woman they would like to live with. She would cook and clean and make him the toast of the town. She has no downsides or bad days. She is all good!

Women have a somewhat different response. They are not so sure they like this woman. For some, she is one of those women you do not want to stand too close to, lest she show up your faults. For others, she is a traitor to the sisterhood. For others still, she is an unattainable goal and source of nagging guilt.

And yet here is the problem: most *women* have only ever heard *men* preach on Proverbs 31. This is probably as it should be, since men should be the teaching elders in our churches. But a few years ago when I spoke on Proverbs 31 at a large women's conference, so many women told me that it was great to hear a woman speak on this text that I came away thinking that even if the sex of the preacher was not really an issue, the perceived gender stereotype was. There was something about men preaching on this text that prevented women hearing the good of it!

So here I am—a woman—opening up Proverbs 31:10-31, in the hope that we can go some way towards reinstating the Proverbs 31 wife as a worthy role model, and making women less terrified of her and more inclined to be like her. At the same time, I hope Christian men will be encouraged to take a fresh (and generous) look at their wives or, if they are unmarried, be challenged to look for a wife who is like her proverbial sister.

Introducing Proverbs 31

Proverbs 31 comes at the end of the book of Proverbs. The book itself is a gathering into one volume of several collections of wise sayings, which probably existed independently of each other before they were put together at some stage in Israel's history. Much of the book comes from King Solomon.

Proverbs 31, however, does not come from Solomon. It comes from another king, King Lemuel, and he tells us it is an oracle his mother taught him (v. 1). We are not given any more information about who he was, but it is possible that both he and his mother were converts to Judaism because we have no existing records of a Jewish king by that name.

The chapter begins with the queen mother's advice to her son, the king, about the dangers of womanising and wine, and about his responsibility to use his position for good (vv. 1-9). In short, she tells him how to be a wise king. The second part of the chapter is a poem that describes the ideal wife a wise man should seek (vv. 10-31).

In the original language this poem is an acrostic, where each line begins with the next letter of the Hebrew alphabet. In that sense, it is the A-Z or complete guide to the ideal wife.

Before we look at the passage there are two things we need to understand about the book of Proverbs.

The first is that Proverbs is a book of wisdom. It is a book that teaches us how to be wise. These days when we say someone is 'wise', it is usually in the sense that they are shrewd and cunning, or streetwise. It is a gut-instinct wisdom that cannot be learned, and which looks after number one. It has no place for God.

But in Proverbs, wisdom *can* be learned—that is why it is written down—and it is not about self-interest. It is about things like justice, truth, hard work, discretion, generosity, faithfulness and love. And at the heart of it all, and essential for being wise, is "the fear of the LORD". We see it right at the beginning of the book where "The fear of the LORD is the beginning of knowledge" (1:7). In fact, "the fear of the LORD" appears around 20 times throughout the book, and it is the foundation of true wisdom and instruction (9:10, 15:33).

In a nutshell, the *purpose* of the book of Proverbs is to make us wise, and to be wise we must first fear God.

So that is its purpose. The second thing to understand is the way that Proverbs sees the world.

I take it we are familiar with the idea that different parts of the Bible are written in different styles, and that understanding the style helps us understand what we are reading. The book of Proverbs uses a style of writing that is popular in the 'wisdom literature' of the Bible. This style tends to understand the world in black and white with no shades of grey, and it sees a strong link between cause and effect.

This means it uses simple categories of opposites—things are either true or false, good or bad, humble or proud, hard working or lazy, wise or foolish, and so on. And the good people are all good and the bad people are all bad, and good things happen to good people and bad things happen to bad people. It is a neat, all-or-nothing world. There are only two ways to live and there is no-one in the middle. And if you choose the right way, everything will turn out right for you.

That is what it is like with the Proverbs 31 wife. In effect, she is the *good* version of the bad version that has appeared repeatedly throughout the book.

The bad version is the 'other woman'. She is an adulteress or prostitute (2:16-19; 5:3-16, 20; 6:23-29; 7:4-23; 9:13-18; 23:27-28; 30:20). She has beauty without discretion (11:22). She is a disgraceful wife (12:4) who destroys her family (14:1). She is a fretful, nagging and quarrelsome wife (19:13; 21:9, 19; 25:24; 27:15). There are two ways to live and this woman chooses the wrong way. There is nothing good about her. She lives for pleasure, destroys families and neglects her responsibilities.

The Proverbs 31 wife, on the other hand, chooses the right way and there is nothing bad about her. She stands in stark contrast to the unwise woman, and *all* the 'bad' characters we meet in Proverbs: the sluggard, the unjust merchant, the neglectful parent, the drunkard, the loose talker, the sinner and the fool, just to name a few.

So after that rather long introduction, here is our text:

> [10]An excellent wife who can find?
> She is far more precious than jewels.
> [11]The heart of her husband trusts in her,
> and he will have no lack of gain.
> [12]She does him good, and not harm,
> all the days of her life.
> [13]She seeks wool and flax,
> and works with willing hands.

¹⁴She is like the ships of the merchant;
    she brings her food from afar.
¹⁵She rises while it is yet night
    and provides food for her household
    and portions for her maidens.
¹⁶She considers a field and buys it;
    with the fruit of her hands she plants a vineyard.
¹⁷She dresses herself with strength
    and makes her arms strong.
¹⁸She perceives that her merchandise is profitable.
    Her lamp does not go out at night.
¹⁹She puts her hands to the distaff,
    and her hands hold the spindle.
²⁰She opens her hand to the poor
    and reaches out her hands to the needy.
²¹She is not afraid of snow for her household,
    for all her household are clothed in scarlet.
²²She makes bed coverings for herself;
    her clothing is fine linen and purple.
²³Her husband is known in the gates
    when he sits among the elders of the land.
²⁴She makes linen garments and sells them;
    she delivers sashes to the merchant.
²⁵Strength and dignity are her clothing,
    and she laughs at the time to come.
²⁶She opens her mouth with wisdom,
    and the teaching of kindness is on her tongue.
²⁷She looks well to the ways of her household
    and does not eat the bread of idleness.
²⁸Her children rise up and call her blessed;
    her husband also, and he praises her:
²⁹"Many women have done excellently,
    but you surpass them all."

^{30}Charm is deceitful, and beauty is vain,
　　but a woman who fears the LORD is to be praised.
^{31}Give her of the fruit of her hands,
　　and let her works praise her in the gates.
　　　　(PROV 31:10-31)

Introducing the ideal wife

Having read the passage, the obvious question is "Who is this poem about?" Chances are that unless you are a love-struck young fellow due to get married in the next few days, there is no-one who immediately springs to mind.

Indeed, because she is just too good to be true, some people think that instead of being a real human being she is really a personification of Woman Wisdom, which is a literary device that has been used earlier in Proverbs (1:20-33, 8:1-36, 9:1-6).

But I am not convinced this is the case. It is not an allegorical way of talking about wisdom. For starters, unlike the 'Woman Wisdom' passages, there is too much detail about this woman's relationships. Besides, this passage is a description, where the other passages are mostly speeches. So although the Proverbs 31 wife displays some of the characteristics of Woman Wisdom, I do not think she *is* Woman Wisdom.

And I certainly do not think, as some feminists do, that the Proverbs 31 wife is a feminine divinity within the Godhead. This is wishful thinking on a grand scale!

Rather, this poem is about the *ideal* wife. A flesh-and-blood woman, who is an historical *possibility* even if she has only ever existed in the ideal!

And as much as she might strike *us* as a counter-cultural picture of womanhood, she was so in the ancient world too. If we look closely we see she is presented as a military hero. This would have been a very novel idea in her day, both because of what it says about her strength and the value of her work, and because songs praising women then, like now, were usually about their erotic physical appeal, not about their domestic prowess.

So what do we learn about this ideal wife?

1. Her worth

The first thing that jumps out in the very first verse is that she is incredibly rare and valuable. Her worth is "far more precious than jewels" (v. 10). No amount of money can buy her and she is almost impossible to find.

The effect of this verse is to make a man want to find such a woman and the subtext is that a woman like this is very, very hard to find.

2. Her choices

A big part of her value is in the choices she makes. That is, her value is not based on who she is before she becomes a wife, but on who she *decides* to be once she is a wife.

She is purposeful and thoughtful and engaged in her life. Her life is not simply happening to her—*she* is making her life happen.

The poem might read as though she is so busy she would not have a moment to stop and think, but what we see is that she is thinking every step of the way. Even though much of her life is set in stone—she is a wife, a mother, a worker and an employer—she still has choices and she uses them wisely.

She *seeks* wool and flax and works with *willing* hands (v. 13). She *considers* a field and *buys* it (v. 16). She *sets about* her work (v. 17, NIV). She *perceives* her merchandise is profitable (v. 18). She *is not afraid* for her household (v. 21). She *laughs* at the future (v. 25). She *speaks* with wisdom and knowledge (v. 26). She *oversees* the affairs of her household (v. 27). She *fears* the Lord (v. 30).

She is not too busy to think! She is a responsible, moral agent. There is no sense that she is her husband's lackey. She has choices, which she makes freely and uses well—for *everyone's* benefit, not just her own.

3. Her character

And what about her character? As a general picture, and especially in the original language, we are told she is a courageous military hero (v. 17). But what else are we told about her character?

First and foremost, she is absolutely *trustworthy* (v. 11). This is why her husband trusts her and has full confidence in her. It should not escape our notice that this is one of the few places in the Bible where trust is placed in anyone other than God. So this is a comment about her God-informed and God-shaped spiritual reliability. It tells us that the heart of what she brings to their marriage is *godly wisdom and character*.

While most of the poem depicts what she does for others without giving us any indication of whether they appreciate her actions, this verse and the final verses see her true praiseworthiness arising from her faith in God. This faith is the foundation of her marriage relationship, which in turn undergirds everything else she does.

But she is not just trustworthy. She is intelligent, thoughtful, industrious and independent. She has an eye for detail. She attends to the needs of others (vv. 15, 21, 27). She is generous and helps the needy (v. 20). She is wise and knowledgeable (v. 26).

And you get the feeling that she is very content with her lot. There is no hint of grumbling. She is not wishing she was someone else or that she lived somewhere else or married someone else or was doing something else. She is getting on with life and enjoying it!

In all these things she shows herself as someone who fears God and who is wise. She is not like the fool, who does not fear the Lord (1:22 with 29), who lacks wisdom and knowledge (1:7, 22; 15:2), who does not plan ahead (6:6-11, 14:16), who is selfish, lazy and greedy (12:24, 27; 15:27; 19:15; 28:25), and who neglects those in need (14:31).

The wise wife knows God's demands on her life and delights in them and obeys them, so she is happy and content.

This can come as something of a surprise to us because we feel exhausted just reading all that she does!

4. Her work

When we come to her work, what is important for us to notice is not the details but two aspects of her work: *where* she works, and the *way* she works.

Firstly, *where* she works: despite all her busyness and the things she is engaged in, it is clear that the primary sphere of her work is her home. That does not mean she never goes out the front gate— at the very least, she is off buying fields and turning them into vineyards—but in terms of where she spends most of her time and where she does most of her work, it is in her home.

She works *at* home and she attends *to* her home. She weaves fabrics and makes clothes for herself and her family and coverings for her bed. She makes sure the entire household is well-fed. And *from* her home, she has built a booming cottage industry that is turning a sizeable profit.

She is not content to do her bit round the home and then spend the rest of her week shopping (online or at the mall) and doing lunch on her husband's income. She uses her home, her gifts, her energies and her time to *work*, and part of that work involves making informed financial decisions about her business and investing her profits.

And of course, this leads us to the *way* she works: she is willing, energetic, planned and resourceful. She does not stay up late because she has been slow getting her chores done. She chooses to stay up late because she enjoys her work and she enjoys the benefits it brings.

She is incredibly productive and the product of her work is top-shelf stuff. She wears fine linen and purple. Her family wear scarlet. They are warm, and they lack nothing.

In fact, her incredible productivity and strength are emphasized by repeated references to her hands and arms and physical strength (31:13, 17, 19, 20), with special reference to their fruitfulness (vv. 16, 31).

She is the opposite of the proverbial sluggard, who plants a field and neglects it (24:30-34), whose hands refuse to work (21:25), and who is too lazy to get out of bed (26:14). In contrast, the Proverbs 31 wife fills every moment of the day productively and refuses to eat the bread of idleness (v. 27). She is a hive of activity.

In contrast to the way we often think about it, we see here that work is a blessing not a curse! God made us to work (Gen 1:28), not to be idle, and finding satisfaction in our work (whether it is paid or unpaid) is a blessing from him (Eccl 2:24-25).

5. Her speech

Like her hands, her mouth also produces good things. She speaks with godly wisdom and teaches with kind instruction (31:26).

Her speech, in fact, is the climax of her achievements, because with it she meets her family's relational, moral and spiritual needs. She is wise, and the content and manner of her speech are proof of it.

Speech is a huge theme in Proverbs, especially the idea that we can know a person by their words. If we ever feel the need to turn God's spotlight of holiness on our speech, there is no better place to start than by reading Proverbs and noting every mention of speech and words. If we did that we would find that the spotlight falls not only on the content of our speech but also how we say it.

It is like this also for the Proverbs 31 wife. Not only is the *content* of her speech shaped by God's wisdom, but also it is *loving* instruction.

We should not be surprised that she teaches. Scripture is clear that women are competent and have a role in teaching. Mothers have a duty and role in teaching their children (Deut 6:7, 21:18;

Prov 1:8, 6:20, 30:17; Song 8:2; 2 Tim 1:5, 3:14-15), and at many times God used women to speak his truth (e.g. Exod 15:20-21; 2 Kgs 22:14-20; Acts 21:9).

If we were in any doubt, these passages make it clear that when the New Testament restricts the authoritative teaching of the church community to suitably gifted men, it is not because women are not capable of teaching. It is because of God's order of relationships. Beyond that context, women can and do teach. They can teach the most vulnerable and suggestible among us—our children. The Lord can also use women to teach in other contexts with other types of speech, like prophecy, singing and prayer (cf. Acts 18:26; 1 Cor 11:4-5; 14:3-5, 24-40; Col 3:16).

Indeed, Proverbs 31 has already reminded us that God uses women to teach. The words of this chapter may be "the words of King Lemuel" (v. 1), but they were really the words of his mother—words he considered to be so wise that he made sure others would have their benefit.

In short, the speech of the Proverbs 31 wife brings good not harm. Her words match her life. They communicate God's truth and they are pure, loving and wise, not hot-tempered, gossipy, quarrelsome or self-seeking. They are all good.

6. Her beauty

Not only does the ideal wife work hard and speak well, she has not neglected herself either. She is physically strong (v. 17) and well-dressed (v. 22). She has strength and dignity (v. 25), the energy of youth and the wisdom of age.

And did you notice that she has paid particular attention to her marital bed, making it soft and comfortable and attractive? Instead of being too busy or too tired to have any sort of sex life, she has used her creativity and her industry to pay special attention to that aspect of her marriage relationship. And she has done much more than dim the lights and put on some music.

She has spent days, if not weeks, selecting fabrics and sewing a beautiful rich covering for their bed.

And by faithfully and lovingly covering her bed, she spoils the appeal of the seductress who lures men to her bed by saying that she has covered her couch with coloured linens from Egypt and perfumed her bed with myrrh, aloes and cinnamon (7:16-17).

These days there are virtual seductresses on every second billboard, website, movie and ad break, who taunt the mono-gamous by awakening desire. A man (or woman) does not have to wander any further than their computer to be caught in the trap of sexual sin, not to mention the appeal of the person at work, the gym or church who "*really* understands me". The temptations today are no less real, even if Egyptian bedding and aloes rarely feature in the allure.

But it seems the Proverbs 31 wife knows that good sex in marriage is not only *good*—it also goes a long way to preventing *bad* sex. And this is a word for us too! It is not enough to extol and expect marital faithfulness and then neglect or deprive each other's sexual needs. As Christian husbands and wives committed to the physical, psychological and spiritual wellbeing of our spouse, we express our love for each other *and* love each other by meeting the other's sexual needs. This both benefits our marriage and deprives Satan of grounds for temptation (1 Cor 7:5; Heb 13:4).

Perhaps despite our busyness, we need to take a leaf out of the Proverbs 31 wife's book and ensure we have time to do a little quilting—or whatever euphemism seems fit.

7. Her relationships

In addition to this private part of her married life, so much else of what the Proverbs 31 wife does is also for her husband. He gains so much from her. He lacks nothing of value (v. 11). She brings him good, not harm (v. 12). She ensures that he and her household do not go hungry or cold (vv. 15, 21). Her competence, hard work and good reputation at the city gate enhance his work and his reputation at the city gate (vv. 23, 31). *Nothing* she does reflects badly on him (*who of us wives can say that?!*).

In the language of Genesis, she is "a helper fit for him" (Gen 2:18, 20). Or in the apostle Paul's words, she is her husband's "glory" (1 Cor 11:7). Or in the words of Proverbs, she is "the crown of her husband" (12:4).

The other focus of her energies is her children. They want for nothing. They are well-fed, well-clothed, wisely instructed, and prepared for any event life might throw at them.

There is no sense that her activities outside the home are compromising her ability to care for her family. In fact, the opposite is true: everything she does outside the home has a positive payoff inside. And as we have seen, her good deeds are not confined to the walls of her home; she is out and engaged in her community, generously caring for the poor.

This is a good place for me to say to those women who are reading this and are currently unmarried—either because you have never married or because you are divorced or widowed—that there are still things to be learned from this woman. She is a *specific* picture of feminine wisdom within a certain set of relationships. But if we take away the *particulars* of her life and look at the principles shaping it, it is not too hard to see how her wise choices, her godly character, her hard work, her true and loving speech, and her faithfulness in relationships have things to teach all of us—not just the married ones (and not just the women!).

8. Her faith

I think many post-feminist women read Proverbs 31:10-31 and feel it is a long way from our experience and expectations of womanhood and marriage. So we get to verse 30 and we sigh with relief. Finally, here is something that is familiar and that makes sense of what we see in the mirror each morning when the creams stop working: "Charm is deceitful, and beauty is vain".

Implicitly, this verse tells us that even the Proverbs 31 wife will lose her looks. It turns out she is human after all!

And verse 30 is true, isn't it? Beauty and social airs and graces are like mist that burns off as soon as the sun comes up. They promise happiness but they cannot last the distance because they are not the stuff of real relationships. They are shallow and transitory. Pity the woman who builds her life on them, or the man who chooses a wife on the basis of them.

What lasts is the fear of the Lord. It counts for something. "A woman who fears the LORD is to be praised"—but what does it mean to fear the Lord?

It does not mean fear in the sense of 'terror' or 'dread', like the fear you have watching a horror movie or when you hear a bump in the night. It means knowing God for who he really is: that he is *the* one and only true God, pure, sovereign, all-powerful, all-knowing, all-loving, the Creator and sustainer of all things, and the only judge and true redeemer. Fearing God means being in awe of him, loving him, trusting him, obeying him—and not just on Sundays but as a day-to-day way of living that springs from a relationship with the living God. To fear God is a daily decision to put him first in our lives.

And that is what lies at the heart of true wisdom.

As we have seen, the ideal wife's spiritual life is not in a different compartment from the rest of her life. In actual fact, her faith in God is the beginning and the foundation of everything else in her life. It is there at the start of the poem and here at the end. Take away her faith and the rest disappears. It is like the key to a car. The most expensive car in the world might look good in the driveway, but if we do not have the key, it will get us nowhere.

She does not work hard to win God's favour or to manipulate him so that her life will be blessed. Her entire life is the way it is because she knows who God is and what he wants of her, and she delights to please him. She is our ideal sister of faith.

9. Her reward

Because she has put her faith in God and not in her own achievements, she is to be praised. She knows that she is nothing without God's help and grace, and so God is pleased with her. Her husband and children and all those who see her praise her *because she fears the Lord*. Because she has given her life over to God and to the service of others, she loses nothing. In fact, she comes off a winner.

She gains dignity and respect, satisfaction and acclaim from her work, confidence about the future, and her husband and children call her blessed. If they could bottle this for Mother's Day, they'd be on to something!

This woman has everything—and it all starts with her faith in God.

Answering her critics

That completes the picture of this ideal wife. But while it is a complete picture in some respects, it is not really a *complete* picture. It says nothing about her emotional life, what her family is like, how much she loves them; nothing about the complexities of life, her frustrations, disappointments, illnesses, ageing parents and so on.

We see glimpses of her relationships with her family, but only at the most functional level. In reality, she is a rather flat picture. So we need to be careful that we do not build too much on it.

We also only get a snapshot of her life. What happens when the kids leave home? What if she cannot have children? What if she cannot find work or she develops a chronic illness?

But even if we keep these limitations in mind, there are three challenges she offers to common attitudes and values.

1. 'A woman's place is in the home'

First, as a woman who runs her own business both from her home and outside her home, she is a problem for those people who want to make blanket rules like 'A woman's place is in the home' and 'Mothers, especially of young children, should not do paid work'.

So what wisdom can she give us on working mothers? There are seven points to make.

(i) She will not let us say that a wife and mother must not work outside the home.

(ii) She will not let us say there is anything intrinsically wrong with a wife and mother having her own finances and making her own financial decisions.

(iii) She will not let us say there is anything intrinsically wrong with a wife and mother owning property or running a business and having and supervising employees.

However:

(iv) Her *main* sphere of operations is clearly her home and her *primary* focus is her family.

(v) Her family only benefit from her work. There is no sense that they are missing out because she is not there when they need her, or that she is too tired for them at the end of the day, or that her house is a mess, the fridge is empty and the clothes all unwashed. Whatever she is doing to earn an income, it fits in around her family responsibilities.

(vi) It must also be said that she is a rich woman. She has maids and wealth and so she and her husband are not trying to make ends meet or pay off a mortgage. He has not lost his job and she is not a single mother. That tells us we cannot just lift her life off the page and impose her life and marriage on our lives and marriages, without looking at what is the same and what is different.

(vii) Having said that, we must notice what she does with her wealth. She meets the needs of her family but she *does not go over the top.* They are comfortable, well-dressed and well-fed, but you do not get the sense that they have the newest top-of-the-range version of everything. And she is generous. She gives to the poor what she does not need for her family or her business. She does not put possessions before people.

Her hard work is driven by her love for God and for those he has given her and so the goal of her labour is not a brick house, two cars, skiing trips and a life of luxury. Her goal is to make the most of everything God has given her, and to use it *all* to fulfil the demands of *all* her relationships —with God, her husband, children, servants, the poor— *all* the time, and for *their* sakes not her own. Which of course is what we all should be doing, whether we are married or not.

So should mothers do paid work? Well, that depends! I think most people agree that *ideally* it is best if children, particularly young children, have mum and dad as their primary carers. And usually the mother has the lion's share of responsibility in that great task (cf. Titus 2:4-5).

However, not everyone's situation is the ideal and so choices have to be made. And there are two key questions that should guide the decisions of mothers (and fathers).

The first is: "Does my work help or hinder me in meeting the needs of the people God has given me to love (spouse, children, parents, friends, Christian brothers and sisters, etc.)?" This includes not just their physical needs, but also their relational and spiritual needs. Can we give them the *time and love* they need?

The second is: "Do I really need the money?" Are we living beyond what we really need? Are we putting money and the nice things money can buy before people and God?

The answers to these questions might not mean that we need to stop work altogether, but they might mean we need to cut back our hours or ambitions or get another job. We might even find that with a bit of rethinking and reprioritizing, much more of our lives can be invested in relationships and ministry.

2. 'More proof that women run the world!'

If the Proverbs 31 wife is a problem for those with a narrow, traditional understanding of motherhood, she is also a problem for feminists, who cannot quite work out whether they like her or they don't!

They all like the fact that she is smart, strong, competent, economically productive, and independent. But some of them think she is the one wearing the pants in the marriage, and the husband is useless and sits at the city gate and gets all the glory. And so she is proof that women do all the work and men get all the glory, and that if women ran the world it would be a better place. For other feminists, the wife seems to be running herself into the ground for the sake of her family and, despite all her strength, is still a domestic goddess of the doormat variety.

Both these views miss the point. This is a song about the ideal *wife*, not *husband*, which is why we only get a glimpse of him. We do not need to know anything about him except that he is blessed by her virtues.

But even then, what we see is that neither she nor he is 'winning'. She benefits from the security, wealth, opportunities and praise he gives her, and he benefits from her godliness, competence, hard work and good reputation. They have sexual intimacy and a spiritual relationship, which bless them both. They do different things, but neither is better off than the other. The marriage is a partnership that is *mutually* beneficial.

3. 'Just what I need—another guilt trip!'

But perhaps, despite all this, as a woman she still makes us feel bad.

After all, we do not live in a world where people are either all good or all bad, and good things happen to good people and bad things to bad people. We live in a messy world where simple categories just do not work, and where the link between cause and effect is not as simple as the book of Proverbs makes out.

Perhaps you have spent years making your husband's life happen, and yet he never thanks you or does anything for you. Or perhaps your children do not even pick up their clothes from the floor, let alone rise up and call you blessed. Or perhaps you are one of the good people that bad things have happened to.

This is where it is so important to understand the *style* of Proverbs. Proverbs gives a simplistic view of life that has to be balanced by other things we see in Scripture.

In other parts of Scripture, we see that what *God* thinks about us is what counts—not what *other people* think about us. It is God's praise that really matters. In that context, it matters that he sees *everything* we do—the things other people see and the things they do not. It matters because he is the one who will judge and reward us as we deserve, just as he will judge everyone for how they have lived their lives (Matt 6:3-4, 6, 17-18; Rom 2:16).

If we look outside Proverbs, we also see that bad things happen to good people and vice versa, and that the connection between what we do and what happens to us is not as watertight as the book of Proverbs might have us think. Just think of Job. But we are also told that God is all-loving and all-powerful and that we can trust him even when the pieces of our lives do not add up. We are told that a day is coming when all the wrongs will be righted and when everything will make sense (Rom 8:18-39).

And of course in the rest of Scripture we also see that none of us is perfect. So we know the Proverbs 31 wife sets an ideal that none of us can achieve this side of the new creation. Not even her.

This is exactly why we need the Lord Jesus as our saviour and king. No matter how hard we try, none of us will be the perfect wife, the perfect mother, the perfect daughter, sister, fiancée, girlfriend or friend, even if we make it our life's work to be so. Likewise for the men—they will never perfectly love their wives or lead their families or honour their parents. *All* of us fall short of God's ideal because we have all rejected him and his wisdom. The only one who can meet God's perfect demands is his perfect Son.

And because of that, we need to *fear God*. We need to fear the one who has the power to throw us into hell (Matt 10:28), but who has also provided our escape in his perfect Son.

When we fear God, as women who have been forgiven and who have received the life-giving transforming Spirit of holiness, the Proverbs 31 wife becomes an encouragement to us—not a threat. No matter what our age or marital status, she becomes a sister in faith; a woman like us, who trusts in God's grace and lives to please him, just as we should.

And for men who know that same forgiveness and Spirit, the Proverbs 31 wife is not a bar that a wife or potential wife must jump over. Rather, she is a reminder that all of us reach our full potential only when we put God first and pour out our lives in the service of others. The Proverbs 31 wife is a sister in the faith who shows men what to desire and cherish in a woman.

A sad story

A number of years ago, I attended the funeral of a woman my age. She was a faithful wife and mother with a young family. She had been an award-winning student with a brilliant career. She had a beautiful, well-kept home and garden, and a wide circle of friends. By all the standards of this world, she was the real deal, the ideal woman. So it seemed natural that her family chose this text for her funeral.

But when it was read, the second part of verse 30 was deliberately left out, because although the rest of the poem fitted this woman, she did not fear God. What a fearful moment that omission was.

Instead of bringing comfort and hope at that point, God's word brought a (silenced) word of judgement. The tragic irony was that if Proverbs 31:10-31 tells us anything, it is that we can spend our lives working our fingers to the bone, being high achievers and devoted family members; we can even work tirelessly for the poor. But if we do not first fear God, all is lost.

10 | BUT DOES IT WORK?

UNLESS YOU HAVE BEEN asleep, you will have noticed that the focus of this book has been on the text of Scripture— text by text, verse by verse and sometimes even word by word. We have not really stopped to consider whether doing ministry and relationships in the way God designed actually works. This book has been a Bible study rather than a personal testimony.

This has been both deliberate and self-conscious.

It is an outworking of my belief that the canonical Scriptures are the Spirit-inspired word of God in which God reveals all we need to know for salvation and to know and please him, and that therefore his written word has priority in deciding all matters of faith and life. It is also an outworking of my belief in the sovereign ability of God to communicate *clearly, consistently and relevantly* in that word.

But this last point begs the question.

You and I know there are those who read the same texts, and even come to similar conclusions about what each text said to the first Christians, and yet who conclude for various reasons that these texts do not apply to us today. If God's word is so clear, so consistent and so relevant, how can this be?

A full answer to this question would require another book! But the short answer is that it has much more to do with us than it does with God's word.

The reality is that we cannot know God's will *perfectly* now— even though he has given us his perfect word. Three things contribute to this reality:

(i)   The natural impediment of our human frailty and limitations means that our knowledge of God and his will is both partial and provisional.

(ii) Our own personalities and experiences provide the context for us hearing, understanding and accepting the truth and wisdom of God's word.

(iii) Our sinful rebellion against God causes us to doubt the goodness and 'liveability' of God's word, and to reject its authority over our lives.

The first of these three factors—that our knowledge of God and his will, while God-given and sufficient, is nevertheless still seeing "in a mirror dimly" (1 Cor 13:12)—does *not* explain why Christians come to opposing conclusions on this or any other matter. But the other two factors certainly do!

None of us reads the Bible as a neutral reader. We are influenced by personal factors and we are influenced by our fallenness— and these influences each amplify the effect of the other. Our fallenness makes us reluctant and less able to spot the influence of our personality and experiences on hearing and understanding God's word, and our personality and experiences obscure the influence of our fallenness to do the same.

Some years ago, I had a conversation with a friend after a meeting in which we had planned a response to a push within our denomination for women to be appointed to full church leadership. Even though my friend was totally convinced we were working to prevent something that was contrary to God's will, she asked a question we should all ask, whichever side of this or any theological debate we are on. It was: "What if we're wrong?"

It is a good question because it recognizes the possibility that we might be wrong! And it is a good question because it forces us to re-examine those things that might prevent us from hearing and understanding God's word correctly.

My answer to my friend was that on the last day *all* of us will learn things—even the smartest, most theologically astute amongst us! On that day, all of us will be 'wrong' about something, but if we trust in Christ we have nothing to fear. In the meantime, we need to do two things that on the face of it may seem contradictory.

On the one hand, we need to recognize the limits of our ability to know God and his will, and work hard at identifying those things—in ourselves and in our society—that work against us hearing and understanding it correctly.

And on the other, we need to have confidence that, in the Bible, God has told us everything we need to know in order to please him. We need to have confidence in God's ability to communicate clearly in the Bible and then we need to search and study it, and prayerfully and humbly get on with obeying it.

It is these two responses—of recognizing my limitations and the obstacles in me to hearing God's word, and recognizing God's sovereign and sufficient provision by his Spirit in that word—that led me to change my mind on the relationships between men and women.

My journey

I began this book saying that I was more surprised than anyone to find myself writing it. Let me explain.

I am old enough to have been raised in the heady heyday of the women's liberation movement. Its impact on my home, my school and broader society was profound—all the more so because I spent half my school years in an exclusive all-girls school, and from my mid-teenage years lived in an all female household (even the pets were female!).

I was raised to think that a woman could do anything a man can do (and she could do it *better*), and that the differences between the sexes were only matters of biology. I believed strongly in a woman's right to control her own body, that women should be allowed the same sexual freedom that men had traditionally 'enjoyed', and that the world would be a better place if women ran it. I recall I had very little respect for men.

And as someone who was passionately anti-Christian, had I known about the texts I have written about in this book, I would have consigned them—along with all that the Bible teaches—to my bonfire of ridiculous beliefs. They would simply have provided more proof, as if it were needed, that Christians were wrong and I was right!

But how wrong I was. Somewhat out of the blue (humanly speaking), God took away my spiritual blindness and gave me saving faith in Christ and his death in my place. God then began deconstructing and renewing everything I had previously believed.

In God's kindness, and probably because he had bigger fish to fry, it was several years before he challenged my beliefs about men and women. In fact, it was several years before I really *noticed* the texts that have occupied us in this book—although I must have read them earlier.

Certainly one reason for this delay is that I ended up at a church that was more committed to the free expression of the 'gifts of the Spirit' than to what the Bible had to say about the exercise of those gifts. In practice, the only requisite for exercising a gift was the ability to do it. So if a person was a gifted teacher of God's word, then that gift was a manifestation of God's Spirit and to prevent that person teaching would have been to quench the Spirit (cf. 1 Thess 5:19). The gender of the speaker and of the hearers was never a factor. I am not sure what they made of texts like 1 Corinthians 14 or 1 Timothy 2, but evidently these texts had no impact on the ministry of women because it was unexceptional for women to preach in the Sunday worship services and even plant and lead churches.

While some of my pre-Christian feminist beliefs were quickly challenged and rejected—chief among them a woman's 'right' to end the life of the unborn—nothing in the practice or teaching of my church challenged my pre-Christian belief that a woman could and should do everything a man can do.

Then, by something of an accident (again, humanly speaking), I came to study theology at an evangelical theological college. This meant taking several steps in a very different direction. The Christian culture was different. The place of Scripture was different. The people were different. While I had loved reading the Bible from the day I was converted, the time and focus spent on careful study of words and texts was new to me. Even then, it was some time before I realized the Bible had things to say about women and men that I had not heard before and needed to hear.

Now, my guess is that you are not reading this book to find out about me. What a relief! But if we need to be conscious of the factors influencing our hearing and understanding of God's word, then it is only fair that you get a glimpse of how I came to hold the views I hold. And the point I am making is that the gravitational pull for me on the question of male and female roles was all in one direction—*and that direction was 180 degrees contrary to the view I have expounded and defended in this book.*

So what made me change my mind?

Well, it would be neat and simple if I could say that just *one* thing changed my mind, and that this one thing was reading, studying and exegeting the Scriptures. But it would not be true.

Having said that, there is no doubt that the impetus to examine this issue came from a growing awareness that my view was very different from what certain Bible passages said, and there is no doubt that Scripture was the single major factor that caused me to change my mind.

The change was gradual. The first time gender issues came into the foreground for me was in the context of the college preaching seminars. Like all first-year students, I was scheduled to preach to a group of my peers so that they could then critique my efforts. My assigned text was from 1 John.

Several weeks before my turn to preach, a few of my male classmates told me of their problems about hearing me preach. They did so graciously and gently, and there was plenty of discussion. Their solution was not to come to the class. But at the same time, one or two of them urged me to reconsider in light of the Scriptures.

I admit these developments took me somewhat by surprise. But since attendance at these seminars was mandatory, and since the text I was to preach on was about love, I withdrew my name from the schedule. I figured I would hardly be acting in love if my brothers had told me of their difficulties and I then insisted on preaching, forcing them not to attend. It was an easy decision and it cost me very little.

As it turned out, it was not such an easy decision for the college.

Some students were angry with those who had questioned my right to preach. For them, it was a matter of justice. Some were angry with me for withdrawing. For them, I had conceded ground in their fight for identical women's ministry. Others raised questions about the nature of the preaching seminars—about whether they involved 'teaching with authority' given they were exercises in learning, more for the benefit of the preacher than the hearers.

The response of the principal, faculty and college student leaders in no small part determined the lessons I learned from it all.

First and foremost they reasoned from, and directed us to, the Scriptures. And so I spent time studying God's word and working out whether or not women were able to do everything men were able to do when it came to teaching the Bible. I spent time working out if the preaching seminars were the same as the setting for the instructions in 1 Corinthians 14 and 1 Timothy 2 or if they were something different, in which case the restrictions did not apply in the same way.

In the end I decided the seminars *were* something different, and so some weeks later I preached to a small group of my peers— brothers and sisters—and a male lecturer, and they gave me kind and valuable feedback.[1]

But there was another standout feature of this incident. It was that those men who treated me *best* as a woman—who cared for me, encouraged me and valued my ministry *as a woman*—were the same men who held a complementarian view of the roles and responsibilities of men and women. And I have observed this same phenomenon many times in the years since this first unintentional foray of mine into the gender debate.

It would be foolish of me to say that all men (and women) holding complementarian views treat women perfectly. They are sinners just like the rest of humanity. But I can honestly say that those men (and women) who have most made me feel that my views and my ministry and my ability to understand God's word are substandard and 'second-class' have been those holding *egalitarian* views, not complementarian.

In particular, they have suggested that I only hold my views

---

1   The college has now introduced single-sex preaching seminar groups for both women and men, in addition to mixed groups, so that all students are able to participate as preachers and critiquers.

because I am told to do so by certain 'men in authority' or in order to preserve the 'power' of my husband, who is an ordained minister. I find these suggestions deeply offensive—not to mention ironic!

They are offensive because they ascribe motives to me when these people do not and cannot know my true motives (cf. 1 Cor 4:4-5). They are offensive because they suggest I am weak and incapable of making up my own mind on this issue. They are offensive because they disregard the years of learning and study I have undertaken to equip me to handle the Scriptures responsibly. They are offensive because they suggest that I lack the Christian integrity to hold views that are different from those around me. And they are offensive because they overlook the fact that the view I hold about God's intentions for men and women has a personal cost: it has meant that my ministry is limited in a way it would not be if I did not hold this view, and it has negatively affected countless precious relationships with friends and family.

And, of course, these suggestions from egalitarians are ironic because they deny me—a woman—the right and ability to make up my own mind, and so they fail to treat me and my views with equal respect. And they reflect a gender-based paternalism that assumes I hold these views only because men told me to. So much for 'egalitarians' (by definition) believing that women have equal rights, abilities and dignity!

The preaching seminar was over 25 years ago, so a lot of water has passed under the bridge since then. And it will be quite clear from this book that my views on men and women in ministry— and marriage, as it turns out—are not what they were. But as I have said, the change was gradual.

To begin with, my studies at theological college gave me the time, opportunity and skills to study Scripture, and to test the various views in the marketplace of ideas for myself. I was aware there were friends and Bible teachers whom I respected on both sides of the debate, and so I could not decide simply by following a trusted leader. My decision could not be based on personalities or even on a track record of reliability. I had to subject every view to the testimony of Scripture, irrespective of whose view it was.

Also, I found there were weak and extreme arguments on both sides of the debate, so I could not decide purely on the strength of 'logic'. Some egalitarians silenced 1 Timothy 2 on the basis of a hypothetical reconstruction of the situation in Ephesus that has no basis in the text. But some complementarians argued that priests must be male so that in the Eucharist they can represent Jesus, which similarly has no basis in the text of Scripture. That is, it was not enough to choose a 'side' and then simply accept everything that 'side' had to offer.

Everything had to be tested by Scripture.

And fortunately, as God would have it, I have had plenty of time and opportunity and need to do this. As a woman in paid ministry, I had to work out what I did and did not think was consistent with God's design for women in the church. As a wife, I have had to work out what it means for me to submit to my husband. As a mother, I had to work out how to raise my son to be a godly man and (God-willing) husband. As a woman with a public teaching ministry, I often get asked to teach on these matters and to defend my views. As someone active in the life of my denomination, I often have to promote and defend my views within the denomination and in the media. And of course, as a Christian woman, I want to know what God's will for me is, and—with his help—I want to obey it as best I can.

This means that over the past 25 years, I have regularly and often returned to study what God's word says about women and men. And the more I study God's word, and the more I read the various arguments used to reject the plain sense of these texts, the more *convinced* I am of the wisdom and clarity of God's word in declaring that he has given men and women different responsibilities in the family and the church; and the more *frustrated* and *saddened* I am by the inadequate approach of those who reject the historic view of the church on these matters.

Whereas the gravitational pull for me was once all towards the view that there were no differences and should be no differences between men and women, the progression of my view has all been in the opposite direction: that God made men and women to be equal and different. And for the most part, it is the study of Scripture that has brought that change. Praise God.

My experience

But it has not just been study of the Bible that has been responsible for this. The Christian life is *lived*, so there are three further things that have helped form me as a Christian woman, and helped form the views I now hold on these matters:

(i)   my experience of partnering with men in ministry
(ii)   my experience as a wife
(iii) my experience as a woman.

Recently I heard a sermon on 1 Timothy 2 where the preacher claimed that Paul would not have prevented women from preaching in church, because it is clear from his other letters that he held women in very high regard. "Paul loved women!" we were told, and the women named in Romans 16 are proof that he saw no difference in the ministries of men and women.

Well, the preacher was half right. Paul did love women, and his letters (Romans 16 included) provide ample evidence that he was not the misogynist he is often accused of being. His letters make it quite clear that he valued the ministry of women. He valued their teaching ministry (2 Tim 1:5, 3:14-15; Titus 2:3-5). He valued their labouring alongside him in the work of the gospel (Rom 16:7, 12; Phil 4:2-3). He valued their financial support and their sacrificial fellowship in Christ (Rom 16:1-2, 3-4, 6, 7, 13, 15; 1 Cor 16:19; 2 Tim 4:21; Phlm 2). He valued women's ministry generally (Col 4:15; 1 Tim 3:11; 5:5, 9-10; 2 Tim 1:5).

But of course the preacher was also half wrong. The fact that Paul loved women and valued their ministry gives us no indication of whether or not women had the same ministry as men. To work that out we must first listen to those places where Paul explicitly addresses the ministry of women, and then consider whatever glimpses of the ministry of women he gives us in his letters.

Much of this book has been doing the first of these. And when we do the second—that is, look at the glimpses of women in ministry in Paul's letters—we see that *nowhere* does Paul say that women taught or led churches, as men did.

Sure, women were co-workers with Paul in the gospel—but we are not told *how*, or *to whom* they ministered. Sure, they were deacons and patrons—but *doing what* we are not told. Even if some male deacons (or servants: *diakonos* in the Greek) had teaching responsibilities in the church, it does not follow that all deacons (male or female) had such responsibilities (1 Cor 3:5; Rom 16:1; Phil 1:1; 1 Tim 3:8, 12; cf. Rom 12:6-7). To claim they did is an argument from silence, and absolutely contrary to those places in the New Testament where the ministry of women is specifically addressed.

The preacher was confusing an appreciation of women's ministry and brotherly love of women with an endorsement of women in all forms of ministry. He saw the two as being the same thing.

But they are not the same thing. Rather, Paul's love for his Christian sisters was what motivated his desire for them to know what God required of them, and how their ministry was to be different from that of men.

I realize there are some women who do not feel loved or valued or supported in their ministry by Christian brothers. This is a great shame. They are made to feel that their contribution to the work of the gospel is second-rate, that ministry to women and children is not quite the 'real deal', and that the 'real' action of ministry takes place in the pulpit and in ordained church leadership. They want to serve Christ full-time in paid employment, but there are no jobs for them unless they do the same thing as men. Their opinions are not heard or sought in their local church or their denomination. Their differences from men are not celebrated or welcomed.

Thankfully, this is not my experience. There have been a few exceptions, but for the most part I enjoy rich fellowship with brothers who love and care for me and value the contribution I make to Christ's church. And those brothers who are most convinced of the equal and complementary roles and responsibilities of men and women are the brothers who *most* value my ministry; who are most generous in their praise, most supportive of my efforts, and most respectful of my opinions. It is these same brothers who are also most gentle and brotherly towards me.

In addition to the care of these Christian brothers, God has blessed me with the excellent love and care of that dear brother who is also my husband, Rob. Over the past 20-plus years, we have struggled and grown together in our understanding of the different roles and responsibilities of husbands and wives. Sometimes we have been more conscious than at other times of the particular demands of our different roles. We have had to work hard at meeting our distinctive responsibilities—his to lead, mine to submit—and to forgive each other when we have failed to love each other by doing so. But despite the ups and downs of two sinners sharing a bed, a house and a family, it has been a rich and blessed experience—for which I thank God!

And following the lead of his father, our young adult son also respects and encourages my public ministry, and notices and appreciates our efforts to express God's design of complementary roles in our marriage.

All these brothers have allowed me to experience the outworking of my views in a way that is positive and affirming. Had this not been the case, it probably would have been harder for me to hold the views that I do. And so I admit that this positive experience has probably influenced the formation of my views and my willingness to hold them.

Of course, such an admission does not make my views invalid, in the same way that negative experiences (had I had them) would not have validated the egalitarian view! I am merely pointing out the sort of critical self-reflection that is necessary when we—as flesh and blood readers—encounter God's word. All of us need to identify those things that might influence our reading and, as much as we can, try to accommodate those influences, so that God's word speaks unhindered.

The other personal factor that has influenced my response to God's teaching about the roles and responsibilities of men and women is that I find it works.

This is the case in marriage, where as individuals my husband and I are richer for accepting God's different purposes for us both, and as a family our home has been happier and stronger the more it has been shaped by them.

This is also the case in ministry, where there has always been an abundance of opportunities to serve Jesus and his people in ways that are biblically appropriate. I have never felt that there is nothing for me to do in Christ's church. Instead, the needs are overwhelming, so the question has never been "Why is there nothing I can do?" Rather, it has been "Of all the many things to do, what can I do best *as the person God has made me*?"

This has seen me involved in pastoral care and counselling, leading Bible study groups (women's groups, and mixed groups with my husband), university campus ministry, participation in church services (in interviews, reading the Bible, leading liturgy and prayer), practical help, Bible teaching and preaching to women's groups and conferences, writing, crèche, lecturing women, sitting on committees and boards, personal and public evangelism, involvement in the media, financial giving, and much, *much* more. In fact, perhaps the only thing that I have not been involved in is music ministry (and for that we should all be thankful).

My point is that I have never felt that I have nothing to contribute. Because of this, as well as being convinced it is not God's will for me to do so, I have never felt the need to teach the Bible to men or to be a leading elder in a church. I have had to ask myself if I wanted to do so—because invitations have come—but making the decision not to do so has not been a difficult one. I realize this is not always the case for some women who say they feel 'called' to those ministries.[2]

My decision has been difficult only when—if I can be brutally honest, brothers—I hear inept preaching from a man. I do not mean your average run-of-the-mill preaching, where the preacher loves the Lord and loves his word but there is something lacking in the power or passion or application of that word. I mean preaching where the clarity of God's word is obscured, or where error is proclaimed as truth, or where the preacher preaches himself and not our wonderful Saviour. It is then that I feel the rub of the different God-given responsibilities of men and women that prevent women from preaching to mixed congregations.

Of course, I realize the pride inherent in such a complaint. And

---

2   As we have seen earlier in the book (in chapter 2), we must always test subjective 'calls' such as these by Scripture.

I realize it is not only women who struggle with poor preaching. But perhaps this is a good place to remind those brothers who are preachers that you serve your sisters, in a way that you do not serve your brothers, by being the best preacher you can be—because if there is no lack in the pulpit, your sisters will be less tempted to want to fill it.

And the experience of my ministry being valued in the church has been repeated in my marriage.

In the early days of our marriage and ministry, an older woman complimented me on a talk I had given to the women of the church, and she asked if Rob had written it. She meant no offence, and I took none. But Rob had not written the talk, and would never dream of telling me what to say or how to say it. While we have always talked about the various projects, sermons and articles we are working on, we have each respected an invisible fence around each other's work. I have never vetted his sermons (as some ministry wives do) and he has never vetted mine. We do our own work, and we deeply respect each other's gifts and ministries.

In fact, Rob willingly makes sacrifices to facilitate and support my ministry—whether that means time alone at home while I am out speaking or at meetings, lengthy trips to the airport to drop or collect me, or restoring me when certain debates take their toll.

His decision to do this has been quite deliberate. When our son was a toddler, there was a significant moment when Rob realized he had married me because I had a heart for ministry, and now that we had a small child, if I was going to do the ministries he believed I was gifted to do, he would have to help make that possible. That is, his responsibility of headship caused him to think about what he could do to enable me to serve Christ's church.

At that time, his solution was to move many of his appointments to our home so that I was able to accept speaking engagements and attend lectures and meetings. At other times since, there have been different solutions. But I have always felt that he values what I do, and although most of my ministry is unpaid, there has never been any suggestion that Rob sees it as a hobby or having any less value to the kingdom of God than his (paid) ministry.

What I am saying here is that *it works*—that the different roles and responsibilities of women and men we have studied in this book have brought meaning, purpose, joy, and opportunities to me as a Christian woman. I have not lost by accepting these differences. I have gained. And for that, I thank God—and I thank those brothers and sisters who have been faithful in fulfilling their part in those differences.

Anyway, enough of me!

My point in sharing so much of my story has been to show how it has provided the context for my reading and hearing of God's word. Some things have worked against me accepting the teaching of Scripture about men and women. Many things have worked for it. Would I have thought differently had my experiences been different? I hope not.

But it is exactly because of personal factors like these, and the influence of our sinful human hearts, that we all must take such care to handle God's word humbly and understand it correctly. And we must heed the warning bells if our preferred interpretation is directly at odds with the actual words of Scripture, or if it puts us at odds with the majority view of Bible-believing brothers and sisters through the centuries before us.

One last objection

There is one last argument we have not yet considered that might justify putting aside all we have seen about the differences between men and women in God's design. It is the 'missional' argument.

This argument goes something like this: sure, the Bible teaches that God designed men and women for different roles and responsibilities, and 20 centuries ago (or even half a century ago) this teaching might have been acceptable. But *today*, it is just too culturally foreign, too abhorrent, too open to misunderstanding to do any good. It puts people off the gospel. Just as Jesus said that it is better to cut off a hand than with both hands be thrown into hell (Matt 5:30, 18:8), so it is better to cut off this 'hand' than consign people to hell because they have stumbled over this teaching.

Now, let us just pause a moment to feel the weight of this argument. It has a gospel focus. It puts people's salvation first. It sounds loving. It seems to reflect God's priorities.

But it will not do.

Even such a well-intentioned argument is no reason to ditch this age-old teaching of God's word, because it forgets that at the heart of all our sin—that sin which took our Saviour to the cross—is the rejection of the goodness and wisdom of God's word, and the willingness to obey it. That is, this argument is in itself an expression of the same attitude to God's will and God's law that first made us enemies of God.

Granted, 1 Corinthians 14 may not be the first text we use in our evangelism, but neither should it be the last. If God's word goes out from him and does not return to him without accomplishing what he purposes it to do (Isa 55:10-11), it might just be that he will choose to bring faith through the hearing of *that* particular word.

In the normal course of events, if we try to convince people of the wisdom and beauty of God's intentions for men and women before they are convinced of the wisdom and power of Jesus' cross and resurrection, we will be pushing a culturally unpalatable barrow up an incredibly steep hill. We will also be trying to sow God's word in human hearts still hardened by sin and unprepared by the Spirit to receive it.

But this is a question of *timing*, not of substance. We cannot change the substance of God's truth to make the gospel more appealing. The gospel is more radical, more counter-cultural, more confronting than anything the Bible has to say about men and women, or wealth, or sex, or whatever! And so it is entirely wrong-footed to think we can silence a 'difficult' part of God's word in order to win souls for Christ. *Christ* is the stumbling block (Rom 9:33; 1 Cor 1:22-24)! And the miracle of faith is that once we trust in Christ, God enables us by his Spirit to see the truth and wisdom and goodness of all his word and his ways.

So, although the matters we have addressed in this book are not Salvation Issues, they are in some sense still salvation issues.

As Christian believers, we know that people are saved through faith in the gospel of Christ crucified and not through obeying the law—not the Sabbath law, not a 'law' about men and women, not any law. But Christ does not free us from the curse of the law so that we can cut and paste from God's word—God's law—to make it suit us, or our culture, better. We are given new life in the Spirit and freed from the bondage of sin precisely so we can be what God wants us to be, not what we want to be.

Surely this is the attitude we see clearly displayed in the Lord Jesus when he prayed, "Not my will, but yours, be done" (Luke 22:42)? Of course, he had no sin from which to be freed, but what was his decision in the garden of Gethsemane if not a decision to trust and obey the sovereign goodness and wisdom of his Father's will?

Jesus submitted to his Father's will, and so must we.

If we resist God's right to rule our lives, if we doubt the goodness of his word, if we use one part of Scripture to silence another part that we find objectionable, then it is a salvation issue—because our attitude to God's word cannot be separated from our attitude towards God himself.

And so as God's children, may we not resist the Holy Spirit. Rather, may we prefer to differ from our fallen world than from his glorious word in the way we live and relate and minister as Christian women and men, and *in all things*.

APPENDIX: RESOURCES USED IN PREPARING THIS BOOK

Note: not all resources listed here accept the complementarian model of relationships for men and women presented in this book.

General resources

- ST Foh, *Women and the Word of God*, Baker, Grand Rapids, 1979.
- WA Grudem, *Evangelical Feminism and Biblical Truth*, Multnomah, Sisters, Oregon, 2004.
- MA Kassian, *Women, Creation and the Fall*, Crossway, Westchester, 1990.
- J Piper and WA Grudem (eds), *Recovering Biblical Manhood and Womanhood: A Response to Evangelical Feminism*, Crossway, Wheaton, 1991.
- WA Grudem (ed), *Biblical Foundations for Manhood and Womanhood*, Crossway, Wheaton, 2002.

Chapter 2: Finding Peace and Quiet (1 Timothy 2)

- GW Knight III, *Commentary on the Pastoral Epistles*, Eerdmans, Grand Rapids, 1992.
- AJ Köstenberger, TR Schreiner and HS Baldwin, *Women in the Church: A Fresh Analysis of 1 Timothy 2:9-15*, Baker, Grand Rapids, 1995.
- AJ Köstenberger, 'Ascertaining Women's God-Ordained Roles: An Interpretation of 1 Timothy 2:15', *Bulletin for Biblical Research*, 7, 1997, pp. 107-44.
- IH Marshall, *The Pastoral Epistles*, T&T Clark, Edinburgh, 1999.

- DJ Moo, 'What Does It Mean Not to Teach or Have Authority Over Men? 1 Timothy 2:11-15', in J Piper and WA Grudem (eds), *Recovering Biblical Manhood and Womanhood: A Response to Evangelical Feminism*, Crossway, Wheaton, 1991, pp. 179-93.
- WD Mounce, *Pastoral Epistles*, Thomas Nelson, Dallas, 2000.
- PH Towner, *The Letters to Timothy and Titus*, Eerdmans, Grand Rapids, 2006.

Chapter 3: Head to head (1 Corinthians 11)

- TR Schreiner, 'Head Coverings, Prophecies and the Trinity: 1 Corinthians 11:2-16', in J Piper and WA Grudem (eds), *Recovering Biblical Manhood and Womanhood: A Response to Evangelical Feminism*, Crossway, Wheaton, 1991, pp. 124-39.
- AC Thiselton, *The First Epistle to the Corinthians*, Eerdmans, Grand Rapids, 2000.
- GD Fee, *The First Epistle to the Corinthians*, Eerdmans, Grand Rapids, 1987.
- DE Garland, *1 Corinthians*, Baker, Grand Rapids, 2003.
- WA Grudem, 'The Meaning of κεφαλή ("Head"): An Evaluation of New Evidence, Real and Alleged', in WA Grudem (ed.), *Biblical Foundations for Manhood and Womanhood*, Crossway, Wheaton, 2002, pp. 145-202.
- WA Grudem, *The Gift of Prophecy in 1 Corinthians*, Wipf and Stock, Eugene, 1999 [1982].
- BW Winter, *Roman Wives, Roman Widows*, Eerdmans, Grand Rapids, 2003.

Chapter 4: The right to remain silent (1 Corinthians 14)

- DA Carson, '"Silent in the Churches": On the Role of Women in 1 Corinthians 14:33b-36', in J Piper and WA Grudem (eds), *Recovering Biblical Manhood and Womanhood: A Response to Evangelical Feminism*, Wheaton, 1991, pp. 140-53.
- DA Carson, *Showing the Spirit: A Theological Exposition of 1 Corinthians 12-14*, Lancer, Homebush West, 1988.

- AC Thiselton, *The First Epistle to the Corinthians*, Eerdmans, Grand Rapids, 2000.
- GD Fee, *The First Epistle to the Corinthians*, Eerdmans, Grand Rapids, 1987.
- DE Garland, *1 Corinthians*, Baker, Grand Rapids, 2003.
- WA Grudem, *The Gift of Prophecy in 1 Corinthians*, Wipf and Stock, Eugene, 1999 [1982].
- BW Winter, *Roman Wives, Roman Widows*, Eerdmans, Grand Rapids, 2003.

Chapter 5: The divine marriage (Ephesians 5)

- AT Lincoln, *Ephesians*, Word, Dallas, 1990.
- PT O'Brien, *The Letter to the Ephesians*, Eerdmans, Grand Rapids, 1999.
- WA Grudem, 'The Meaning of κεφαλή ("Head"): An Evaluation of New Evidence, Real and Alleged', in WA Grudem (ed.), *Biblical Foundations for Manhood and Womanhood*, Crossway, Wheaton, 2002, pp. 145-202.
- GW Knight III, 'Husbands and Wives as Analogues of Christ and the Church: Ephesians 5:21-33 and Colossians 3:18-19' in J Piper and WA Grudem (eds), *Recovering Biblical Manhood and Womanhood: A Response to Evangelical Feminism*, Crossway, Wheaton, 1991, pp. 165-78.

Chapter 6: Won without a word (1 Peter 3)

- WA Grudem, 'Wives like Sarah, and the Husbands Who Honor Them: 1 Peter 3:1-7', in J Piper and WA Grudem (eds), *Recovering Biblical Manhood and Womanhood: A Response to Evangelical Feminism*, Crossway, Wheaton, 1991, pp. 194-208.
- WA Grudem, *The First Epistle of Peter: An Introduction and Commentary*, IVP, Grand Rapids, 1988.
- JR Michaels, *1 Peter*, Word, Waco, 1988.

Chapter 7: The original man and woman (Genesis 1-3)

- C Ash, *Marriage: Sex in the Service of God*, IVP, Leicester, 2004.
- H Blocher, *In the Beginning: The Opening Chapters of Genesis*, trans. DG Preston, IVP, Downers Grove, 1984 [1979].
- D Kidner, *Genesis: An Introduction and Commentary*. IVP, Leicester, 1967.
- RC Ortlund, 'Male-Female Equality and Male Headship: Genesis 1-3', in J Piper and WA Grudem (eds), *Recovering Biblical Manhood and Womanhood: A Response to Evangelical Feminism*, Crossway, Wheaton, 1991, pp. 95-112.
- BA Ware, 'Male and Female Complementarity and the Image of God', in WA Grudem (ed.), *Biblical Foundations for Manhood and Womanhood*, Crossway, Wheaton, 2002, pp. 71-92.
- GJ Wenham, *Genesis 1-15*, Word, Waco, 1987.

Chapter 8: The ultimate distortion
Online resources

- General: www.theline.gov.au/home
- General: www.relationships.org.au/relationship-advice/relationship-advice-topics/relationship-difficulties/violence-and-abuse-in-relationships
- For male victims: www.oneinthree.com.au/
- Description of the common cycle of abuse: www.dhcs.act.gov.au/hcs/policies/domestic_violence_policy#cycle

Chapter 9: The ideal wife (Proverbs 31)

- D Kidner, *Proverbs: An Introduction and Commentary*, IVP, Leicester, 1988.
- RE Murphy, *Proverbs*, Thomas Nelson, Nashville, 1998.
- BK Waltke, *The Book of Proverbs: Chapters 15-31*, Eerdmans, Grand Rapids, 2005.
- A Wolters, *The Song of the Valiant Woman: Studies in the Interpretation of Proverbs 31:10-31*, Paternoster, Carlisle, 2001.

 matthiasmedia

Matthias Media is an evangelical publishing ministry that seeks to persuade all Christians of the truth of God's purposes in Jesus Christ as revealed in the Bible, and equip them with high-quality resources, so that by the work of the Holy Spirit they will:

- abandon their lives to the honour and service of Christ in daily holiness and decision-making
- pray constantly in Christ's name for the fruitfulness and growth of his gospel
- speak the Bible's life-changing word whenever and however they can—in the home, in the world and in the fellowship of his people.

It was in 1988 that we first started pursuing this mission, and in God's kindness we now have more than 300 different ministry resources being used all over the world. These resources range from Bible studies and books through to training courses and audio sermons.

To find out more about our large range of very useful resources, and to access samples and free downloads, visit our website:

www.matthiasmedia.com

How to buy our resources

1. Direct from us over the internet:
  – in the US: www.matthiasmedia.com
  – in Australia and the rest of the world:
    www.matthiasmedia.com.au

2. Direct from us by phone:
  – in the US: 1 866 407 4530
  – in Australia: 1300 051 220
  – international: +61 2 9223 4627

> Register at our website for our **free** regular email update to receive information about the latest new resources, **exclusive special offers**, and free articles to help you grow in your Christian life and ministry.

3. Through a range of outlets in various parts of the world. Visit **www.matthiasmedia.com/contact** for details about recommended retailers in your part of the world, including www.thegoodbook.co.uk in the United Kingdom.

4. Trade enquiries can be addressed to:
  – in the US and Canada: sales@matthiasmedia.com
  – in Australia and the rest of the world: sales@matthiasmedia.com.au

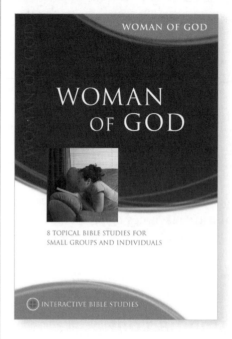

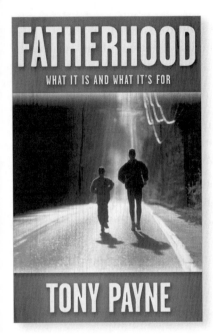

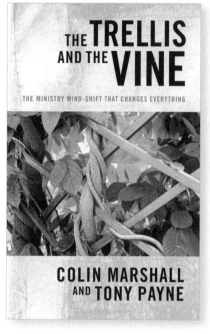

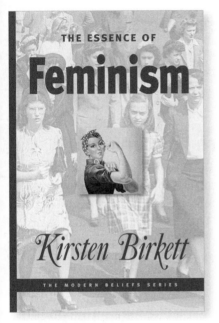

Looking for something more?

If you're looking for more input for your Christian life and service, take a look at *The Briefing*.

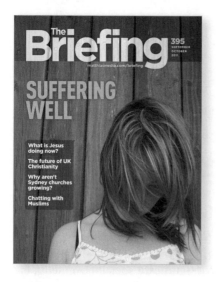

more diversity

With a variety of columns and sections, and local and overseas perspectives, *The Briefing* offers plenty to readers in various stages and walks of life.

more content

Since *The Briefing* is available not just in print but also online, we can provide lots of content, including audio/video and new hosted blogs by gifted Christian thinkers and writers. Choose the content that is most relevant and useful to you.

more convenient

You can receive *The Briefing* in the way that best suits your reading habits—on the web, as an RSS feed, by pdf, as an email update, on your phone or smart device, and of course in print.

more social

Being online, *The Briefing* is share-able and discuss-able. So it's simple to connect your friends into *The Briefing* content via your favourite social networks.

more free

The remarkable thing about *The Briefing* is that it is *all* available free. Of course, if you want to have the beautiful paper edition mailed out to you then there is a small charge.

more information?

All the information you're likely to need, including subscription options, can be found at:

www.matthiasmedia.com/briefing